RRL Publishing

813-885-9097

Publishing@RedRockLeadership.com

RedRockLeadership.com/TheBook.com

ISBN: 978-0-578-63197-4 (print)

Ordering Information:

Special discounts are available on quantity purchases by corporations, associations, and others. For details, contact:

RRL Publishing
Tampa, FL
813-885-9097

Publishing@RedRockLeadership.com

RedRockLeadership.com/TheBook.com

The team at RedRock is available to train your company in leadership! Please contact training@redrockleadership.com for more details.

Transform Your Company Culture and Unleash the Potential for Exponential Growth!

JEFF RUBY

RRL
Publishing®

This book represents a milestone in my life. Writing it has afforded me the privilege of being able to reflect back and recognize the positive impact that my mom and dad and mentors and coaches have had on me throughout the years.

My highest gratitude belongs to my clients. Your success has been the main source of my inspiration. Thank you for allowing me to have a front-row seat to witness your tremendous accomplishments.

Many thanks to you, the reader, for caring enough about those around you to be a student of leadership. This work has allowed me to use my 20 years of experience to fulfill my desire to be a leader who grows companies by growing people.

A very special thanks to my daughters, Erin and Katie, who have inspired and encouraged me along the way. Most especially, I want to thank my amazing wife, Tracey, who continuously supported me with her love and prayers as I endured many long days and nights working to build the business and write this book.

Finally, I am most grateful for God whose grace is unexplainable. He has taken an ordinary man like me and magnified his efforts and abilities. My hope is that He is glorified through my accomplishments.

Jeff Ruby

ENDORSEMENTS

"Jeff Ruby's a master at transforming the culture of a business by teaching a leadership style that embodies compassion and respect for employees at all levels of the organization. This book is a gift for those looking to build a 'culture of caring.'"

—James H. Ruhlman, Executive VP, Michigan Sugar Company

"I love the topic of emotional intelligence as it relates to how people lead and behave at work. Jeff Ruby takes that principle and amps it up to a new level. This book cuts to the chase on holding managers accountable for the social skills they exhibit, how they treat their people, and how this shapes an organization's culture."

—Diane Stern, Vice President HR, InterDent Service Corporation

"Jeff's real-life stories of businesses he has helped provide easy-to-understand examples of how to implement commons ense ideas. I highly recommend this book to, not only new business leaders, but also to those who have been in business for years."

—Dave Kolbe, President, Kolbe Construction

"Jeff Ruby has a fresh approach and energy that is different from other authors and speakers. He shares meaningful stories and examples from his experience leading and coaching teams. If you'll take time to read it, I'm confident that you'll get something great out of this book."

—Robin Moch, Partner, M.E. Wilson Company

CONTENTS

INTRODUCTION

"We aren't being heard."

Two young women had approached me at the end of the first day of RedRock Leadership training. They were obviously incredibly smart, passionate about their jobs, and frustrated by their bosses. Without some sort of intervention, I could see it was highly likely that they would end up seeking employment somewhere else.

I hear this sentiment at almost every one of my leadership training sessions. Because it's so widespread, you may have encountered this yourself. There's a systemic gap to bridge in almost every organization. It's a push-pull between *"Do your job"* and *"I have an idea how we can do it better."*

To some extent, this push-pull has always existed, but today the divide seems larger. Those on the frontline make demands for what looks to be unnecessary change to make their jobs easier. At the same time, those in charge appear to be fixed in their ways and refuse to listen. What's unfortunate is that if this tension is not addressed properly, it reaches a breaking point. Sometimes skilled people on our teams are just not in the right company, but sometimes they are and they leave. There are a lot of reasons behind this tension, but the solution is actually fairly simple.

Leadership training is in high demand right now because it's being recognized as a solution to this very issue. Poor leadership—not just at the top but throughout organizations—is why good companies are failing to attract and keep talent. It's stifling the careers of young team members who aren't acquiring the skills they need to succeed. It's creating a staff of dejected individuals who don't want to be there. It's hurting the bottom line.

This tension might be hurting your company too.

Why is there such a crisis? It comes down to three key elements of a healthy company culture: trust, perseverance, and collaboration.

The heroic, top-down style of leadership introduced by the Baby Boomers and Gen Xers isn't working for Millennials and Gen Zers, who are taught the value of collaboration at every stage of their education. Everything from group projects in the classroom to family meetings that encourage youth to speak their minds and be valued have paved the way for wide-ranging discussions and open doors. Then they enter the work force where top-down leadership is still predominant, and it feels stifling and unsatisfying.

It can be that simple.

People want to contribute on a personal *and* organizational level. The overall outcome matters to those in charge just as it does to those on the frontline. That's the good news. The bad news is that a lack of trust and perseverance is hindering collaboration. It takes both parties being trained properly to lift this dark cloud of confusion.

Company culture matters now more than ever.

The influencers of today's business culture crave truth and understanding. Like never before, people are choosing purpose over money and status. They want to be part of something greater than themselves.

That's why RedRock's Personal and Managerial Leadership training has been so incredibly effective in helping transform company cultures. From our Florida headquarters, we provide training and consulting services to organizations who want to improve their sales and leadership performance. Our training is provided through live workshops and boot camps both from our RedRock Leadership training centers and our clients' locations. We also facilitate mastermind groups and strategic planning sessions, as well as provide how-to videos, articles, and tools that help our clients grow and improve their bottom lines.

What's unique about RedRock Leadership is that our training and consulting services are grounded in the competencies of emotional intelligence, which means that we always start by getting people to look inward to establish a foundation for personal leadership before growing outward. Establishing that personal foundation and understanding creates strong roots so that timely growth can occur.

In this book, you'll find real-life examples of people who are just like you, in organizations just like yours, who entered this training, embraced it, and came out winners. If you'll take the time to learn and apply the principles and concepts outlined in this book, like so many others have, you'll unleash the potential for exponential growth.

Regarding personal leadership, you'll learn to:

- Build and sustain mental toughness and become more emotionally intelligent.

- Forge positive relationships by becoming more personally and socially aware.

- Create actionable goals that match your life priorities and vision for the future.

- Leverage your time to accomplish all that is necessary to reach your goals.

Regarding managerial leadership, you'll learn to:

- Motivate your team so they become autonomous and take immediate responsibility.

- Coach your team to enhance personal, job, and strategic performance skill sets.

- Hold your team accountable for being trustworthy and remaining committed.

- Build a culture of trust that attracts and retains the right talent for your organization.

Having hands-on experience, I'm often called upon to share my personal experiences to help companies grow and individuals overcome the challenges that keep them from accomplishing their personal goals. I am driven to making the kind of impact necessary to create permanent change. My clients are located all over the world and range from sole practitioners to Fortune 500 companies. I've even had the privilege of creating training programs for teens and have found these trainings to be extremely effective when delivered through multiday leadership training camps.

I've always had an entrepreneurial spirit and a desire to help others. At the age of 10, I was building soda can lamps and selling them to my neighbors for a profit. After graduating from The University of Akron, I was named head of sales for a national lighting contractor where I helped grow revenue from $700k to $5.8m in less than four years..

At 30, I started my first company and learned firsthand how poor planning and lack of leadership can bring a company to its knees. It was during that time that I learned the value of being surrounded by solid mentors. Under their guidance I set some lofty goals. Then, once those goals were accomplished, I sold the company and relocated my family from Northeast Ohio to Florida.

In 2010, amidst the ashes of the Great Recession that turned the economy and the business landscape upside down, I founded RedRock Leadership. Since then, I estimate that RedRock has helped strengthen thousands of business leaders around world.

This book is the result of more than a decade of teaching, revising, and updating our training to become one of the most powerful and effective leadership resources around. Jim Ruhlman, executive vice president of Michigan Sugar Company, calls RedRock Leadership training "a game changer."

Your organization can be filled with engaged team members who seek to improve the overall success and profitability of your company. When you develop people at every level, you'll realize a renewed energy throughout your organization.

You're about to take the first step toward transforming your company culture and unleashing the potential for exponential growth. Go to RedRockLeadership.com/the-book. Here you'll find tools and resources that are referred to throughout the book. I'm proud of you for opening this book and taking this important step toward your personal and professional development. I wish you all the best as you embark upon this journey. Here's to your success!

CHAPTER 1

THE IMPACT OF THE FURIOUS PACE OF CHANGE

It doesn't matter what generation we're talking about, every kid grows up with the desire to earn a living and have an impact. My generation had paper routes. My grandfather made money as a kid at the speakeasies. I have clients today whose kids sell vintage Air Jordans on eBay and make a killing. All generations have that same desire to do something; the only differences are changes in the influencers and the popular culture, and that change is happening faster than ever.

It feels like we accomplish more today in one year than ever before. It wasn't that long ago when doing research meant heading to the library to dig into an encyclopedia or actually talking to other people. It's unheard of today, but business used to involve massive collaboration that was fueled by relationships. There was a time when people would pick up the phone and call each other when they needed to figure things out. Networking events were more popular, as was cold calling potential clients. But who does that anymore now that the focus is on social media, which has taken over our lives and our communication? With everything we need available at our fingertips, we've created a society that's grown awfully comfortable with instant gratification. We don't wait for anything, not even information. Everything we want is a click away so it's easy to lose sight of the bigger picture.

Simply put, I think our culture has turned its focus inward. Technology may go far in helping us become more connected but it also creates distance between us. That distance has made our personal lives and our businesses more impersonal. It's not just about being mean or being nice. It's about a lack of personal awareness and loss of empathy.[1] In many ways, we've become less compassionate and less considerate.

The University of Michigan conducted a 30-year study (from 1979 to 2009) of about 14,000 college students that revealed most of today's college students rate themselves as less empathetic than college students did in the 1980s and 1990s.

The results were surprising: About 75 percent of students today rate themselves as less empathetic than the average student 30 years ago. We take relationships for granted because we are inclined to think that we don't need them anymore.[2]

When the nature of business started to change, what I was doing at RedRock Leadership had to change as well. To stay relevant and effective, we had to embrace that change. Our core values as a company remained the same, but our training techniques and coaching methods progressed to meet the challenges and obstacles of today's organizations. Here are the top concerns we hear about from our clients:

---

1 https://www.scientificamerican.com/article/what-me-care/
2 https://www.eurekalert.org/pub_releases/2010-05/uom-ecs052610.php

- Undefined Culture
- Inexperienced People in Leadership Roles
- Interpersonal Conflict
- Lack of Courage
- Succession Planning Issues
- Inability to Manage Time
- Lack of Effective Systems and Processes
- Poor Hiring Skills
- Low Trust
- Low Motivation
- Too Much Criticism and Not Enough Coaching

Why do the main challenges we face in business always seem to come down to people and how they interact with each other? Something big is happening that is causing a lot of disruption today, regardless of your business model.

The Impact of Six Generations

Today, more than ever, we feel the impact of six generations of people who, in their own unique ways, influence our business culture. Pew Research Center has documented much of what we know about them.[3] When attempting to right the ship or create a culture shift within your company, you want to make sure you know how you and the people you work with have been influenced over the years.

---

3 http://www.pewresearch.org/fact-tank/2018/03/01/defining-generations-where-millennials-end-and-post-millennials-begin/?amp=1

THE GREATEST GENERATION

Born between 1901 and 1927, The Greatest Generation (a term coined by journalist Tom Brokaw) was raised in a tumultuous era marked by war and economic depression.[4] Despite its challenges, this generation helped defeat Hitler and build the American economy while making advances in science and establishing government programs such as Medicare.

Influences	<ul><li>Influenza pandemic of 1918</li><li>WWI</li><li>Stock market crash</li></ul>
Traits	<ul><li>Humble</li><li>Personally accountable</li><li>Strong work ethic</li></ul>
Views	<ul><li>Money: Financially prudent/frugal</li><li>Education: A privilege</li><li>Management: "I'll do whatever it takes"</li></ul>

---

4 https://gosmallbiz.com/can-learn-greatest-generation/

TRADITIONALISTS

These are people born between 1928 and 1945. This generation is known as the "Silent Generation," which was derived from the idea that, as kids, they were encouraged to be seen and not heard. It proved to be a fitting description.

Influences	• The Great Depression • WWII • D-Day
Traits	• Loyal • Respectful of authority • Stubborn • Dependable
Views	• Money: Hide it and pay cash • Education: A privilege • Management: "Tell me what to do"

BABY BOOMERS

Born between 1946 and 1964, Baby Boomers grew up with traditional families whose fathers went off to work while the moms remained at home to take care of the house and raise the children.

Influences	• Vietnam • 1960s • Civil Rights movement • Traditional family unit
Traits	• Well-educated • Questioning of authority • Good teamwork skills
Views	• Money: Buy now and pay later • Education: A birthright • Management: "I know best"

GENERATION X

Generation X is a term that was popularized by Douglas Coupland in his 1991 novel, *Generation X: Tales for an Accelerated Culture.* Born between 1965 and 1980, they saw what their parents went through during the ups and downs of the 1970s and 1980s and vowed that they weren't going to repeat the cycle. Gen X also represented the first daycare generation. Many of them were "latchkey kids" who returned from school to an empty home with little supervision because their parents were at work.

Influences	• MTV • Dual-income home • Ronald Reagan • End of the Cold War
Traits	• Independent • Family-focused • Hard-working • Critical of others • Intolerant of bureaucracy
Views	• Money: Cautious and conservative • Education: A tool to get ahead • Management: Seeks a hero

GENERATION Y (MILLENNIALS)

This is the generation born between 1981 and 1996. They're known as "The Trophy Generation" because most of their parents insisted that in any competition, win or lose, they should receive a participation trophy at the very least.

Millennials are confident, ambitious, and goal-oriented, and they have high expectations of their employers. Because of the way they were raised, they tend to seek out new challenges and aren't afraid to question authority.

Influences	• Doting parents • 9/11 • Video games • School shootings
Traits	• Fast-paced • Think like entrepreneurs • Value relationships • Highly mobile • Obsessed with information
Views	• Money: Earn to spend • Education: A necessary investment • Management: An obstacle to moving up

GENERATION Z

Generally speaking, Generation Z includes those born between 1997 and 2012. True digital natives, they've been exposed to the internet, social networks, and smartphones their entire lives. Gen Z is a hyper-cognitive generation who are extremely comfortable with researching and collecting data from many sources all at the same time. To them, the integration of virtual and offline experiences is the norm.

A recent study[5] [6] [7] [8] reveals four core behaviors of Gen Zers, all anchored in one element: their search for truth. In contrast, the previous generation of the Millennials got their start in an era of economic prosperity, which gave them the luxury to focus on themselves. While Millennials will tend to be more idealistic and less willing to accept diverse points of view, Gen Zers value individual expression and want to avoid being labeled or labeling others.

Influences	• The Great Recession • ISIS • Sandy Hook • Obama • The rise of populism
Traits	• Seeks truth • Values freedom of expression • Open to understanding differences in people
Views	• Money: Live life pragmatically • Education: A necessary investment • Management: "Please dialogue with me, don't confront me"

5 https://www.mckinsey.com/industries/consumer-packaged-goods/our-insights/true-gen-generation-z-and-its-implications-for-companies
6 http://www.Millennialmarketing.com/2018/03/the-birth-years-of-Millennials-and-generation-z/
7 https://www.forbes.com/sites/deeppatel/2017/09/21/8-ways-generation-z-will-differ-from-Millennials-in-the-workplace/#435f25a376e5
8 https://www.pewresearch.org/topics/generations-and-age/ions-and-age/

It's critical to understand the differences between these generational cultures and what drives us today. This awareness not only helps us in our everyday lives as we interact with young and veteran colleagues, but it also plays a pivotal role in fixing issues in your organization and ensuring that the people around you remain engaged and motivated.

How Culture Is Being Redefined

I grew up playing sandlot baseball and backyard football during the day and in organized recreation leagues in the evening. It's what I did for fun and how I made friends, but it doesn't seem like kids play sports the same way today. They have so many more options with a growing number of camps, clinics, trainers, and travel teams. These choices complicate things because instead of parents saying, "Get out there and play," they say, "Get in the car. I've got to get you and your brothers and sisters to practice."

Let's face it, parents today are under extraordinary pressure to buy all the gear, shell out money for trainers, and get their kids into the best programs—all before many of them even reach high school. Professional scouting begins as early as middle school, and despite the low odds of success, it becomes an all-consuming pursuit. What happens is that some people get left behind. I realize I'm talking about sports here but the same can be said for dancing, acting, singing, etc.

Today, I happen to coach recreational baseball for teenagers who are not involved in competitive sports. We don't keep score and everyone is recognized at the end of the season. When I first started coaching, I have to be honest, it felt like it was a colossal waste of time. Who doesn't keep score? But I started to recognize you can teach more character-building skills than you can when you're teaching kids how to beat up on their opponents to get themselves to the top. I'm all about competition, but I've noticed when there is less pressure to be a strong individual, I can teach them how to have fun and compete as a team. Ultimately, this sets up a foundation for leadership skills they can use later in their lives.

You see, whether you're playing baseball competitively or just for fun, nobody likes to strike out. But when they do, I'm adamant about helping my players turn what seems to be a negative into a positive. I teach them that baseball is a team sport, so if they strike out, they take what they learned about the pitcher back to the dugout to help the other players out when it's their turn to step up to the plate. If you can get them to stop thinking about themselves, you can help create stronger minds and build leaders.

In my 20 years of coaching, I've worked with Millennials and Gen Zers. It's been interesting, to say the least.

Before the start of last season, I asked my friend if his son, Kevin, a Gen Zer, was going to play baseball but he just shook his head.

"No, no, no. My son doesn't play sports."

"Well, why not?" I asked.

"He tried to play basketball one year, but it didn't work out."

"What happened?"

"He had a bad experience with a coach."

"Bad experience? How so?"

"One day before practice, the coach told him that he needed to do a complete set of 10 push-ups. Kevin told him he couldn't do 10 push-ups at one time, and the coach said, 'If you can't do a complete set of 10 push-ups, you'll never be strong enough to play basketball.'"

Apparently, Kevin took that statement literally and checked out. He told his dad he didn't want to play basketball. My friend didn't push back or tell him to stick with it; he immediately pulled him off the team, and Kevin went back to playing video games because that's what he was comfortable doing.

I told my friend, "Why doesn't Kevin take another crack at sports? Have him come out and play baseball with me. My style is a little different."

Kevin showed up and gave it another shot, but I'm not exaggerating when I say that the poor guy was all thumbs. That first day, it didn't look like he had an athletic bone in his body. But that isn't unusual for someone who's never really played organized sports.

I don't know Kevin's previous coach but I quickly put two and two together. The former coach was either cut from a sports team himself when he was younger or perhaps he was an exceptional athlete who actually responded positively when he was criticized. Either way, I'm sure he had the best intentions. Maybe he saw a bit of himself in Kevin and he just wasn't focused on Kevin as much as he was focused on himself. While his approach may have worked with someone else, it didn't work with Kevin, who was the type of kid who needed to talk things out as he learned about himself and his identity.

Some may argue there's nothing wrong with the coach's approach. You might especially think this way if you heard your parents and coaches tell you to "suck it up, buttercup," "get back in there and play the game," or "keep crying, and I'll give you something to cry about!" when you were a kid.

While confrontation may work to motivate some people, it can also have the opposite effect, causing people to shut down and go in a completely different direction. This is especially true today. Kevin actually believed he would never be strong enough. And I'll tell you this: regardless of your age, generation, or stage of life, when you quit something because someone said you couldn't do it, you're in dangerous territory.

Because of my prior knowledge of the situation and my experience as a teenager, I took a different approach with Kevin. Instead of confronting him about his lack of baseball skills, I approached him with empathy. You see, I was cut from my high school baseball team. Remembering what it felt like, I put myself in Kevin's shoes and focused on encouraging him, not discouraging him.

First, I showed him how to wear a glove. Then I showed him how to catch the ball. I was only about 10 feet away when I threw the ball to him the first time, but I made sure to tell him "good job" and compliment him when he caught it. I could see the light bulb go off in his head. Wow! This isn't so hard after all!

Still, I could tell that Kevin was embarrassed every time he tried to throw the ball or swing the bat, so I immediately started pointing out the positives. During a water break, I pulled him aside and told him, "You have great potential and a natural ability."

"Really, you think so?" It was clear that he had never heard that before.

"I know so."

During our first game, Kevin came up to bat and fouled off the first pitch. He ended up striking out, which wasn't unexpected. When he returned to the dugout, I gave him a high five. I told him, "Man, do you see what you did? You put a charge into that foul ball. Getting the bat on the ball is half the battle, and you did it!"

I knew if Kevin stuck to it, he was going to get a hit. Slowly, over time, Kevin's attitude began to change. That allowed him to improve. No joke, by the end of the season, he was one of our better players. He moved up to the front of the batting order, and he was hitting balls over the infielders' heads like it was nobody's business. Some people would call it a miracle that a kid like Kevin could improve the way he did. But it's not a miracle, and it really isn't unusual at all. It happens every day when someone like Kevin has another person in his corner encouraging him and pointing him to a positive future.

Similarly, this is where so many go wrong in business. When we hire people, we assume they think the same way we do. Then because we don't always take the time to understand them, we don't lead them properly.

Companies like Ernst & Young and Accenture report that Millennials make up more than two thirds of their employees[9] and they're quickly rising to leadership roles.[10] In 2014, Millennials

---

9 https://www.inc.com/jason-albanese/four-ways-millennials-are-transforming-leadership.html?cid=search

10 https://www.inc.com/jason-albanese/3-simple-habits-that-will-make-you-a-better-business-leader.html

represented a majority of the workforce with more than half of them in management.[11]

Here are some quick facts about Millennials (and some about Gen Zers) from recent studies:

- 69% believe office attendance is unnecessary on a regular basis. [Cisco]

- 56% won't work at a company if they ban social media access. [Cisco]

- 80% said they prefer on-the-spot recognition over formal reviews and feel that this is imperative for their growth and understanding of a job. [Achievers and Experience Inc.]

- They have about the same level of organizational commitment as Boomers and Gen Xers. [Strategy+Business]

- 92% believe that business success should be measured by more than just profit. [Deloitte]

- Millennials say they don't deserve special treatment and are equally as committed as non- Millennials. [PwC]

- 41% of Millennials do what their managers tell them to do, which is more than older generations. [Strategy+Business]

- 81% of Millennials have donated money, goods, or services. [Walden University and Harris Interactive]

11 https://www2.deloitte.com/content/dam/Deloitte/us/Documents/about-deloitte/us-millennial-majority-will-transform-your-culture.pdf

- More than 63% of Millennials have a bachelor's degree. [Millennial Branding/PayScale]

- The average tenure in a job for Millennials is two years. (Five years for Gen X and seven years for Baby Boomers.) [Millennial Branding/PayScale]

- They are more politically progressive than any other age group in modern history. [Millennial Branding/PayScale]

- They think like entrepreneurs. [Pew Research Center]

- They are globally oriented. [Pew Research Center]

- They have received more education than previous generations. [Pew Research Center]

- They are more racially and ethnically diverse than previous generations. [Pew Research Center]

Today, more than 50% of the global workforce is comprised of Millennials and Gen Zers.[12] Due to sheer numbers, Millennials and Gen Zers have an extreme impact on today's business culture. I've worked with individuals and companies from all over the United States and as far away as South America, Israel, and India. Across the globe, I've found there are as many generational similarities as there are differences. If not managed properly, generational diversity can be an overwhelming challenge for businesses who want to grow.

For example, Gen Xers grew up during the Cold War, while Gen Z has never known life without a smartphone and the internet. For that reason, and several others, it's important to consider how

---

12 https://www.inc.com/jason-albanese/four-ways-Millennials-are-transforming-leadership. html?cid=search; https://www.inc.com/peter-economy/the-Millennial-workplace-of-future-is-almost-here-these-3-things-are-about-to-change-big-time.html

these differences affect the way you run your business and lead your people.

What You Need to Know About Generational Diversity

People often assume generational diversity causes problems and leads to unnecessary drama. We've gotten countless calls from frustrated Baby Boomers and Gen Xers who are concerned about their Millennial team members. One common concern is that they don't trust them and fear they might leave at a moment's notice.

This concern isn't completely unwarranted. A 2016 LinkedIn study found Millennials will change jobs an average of four times in their first decade out of college while Gen Xers only changed jobs twice in the same period. Another study, conducted by PayScale, shows the average job tenure for a Millennial is two years, five years for a Gen Xer, and seven years for Baby Boomers. The question for these frustrated business owners is this: Why aren't Millennials sticking around?

Here are some of the other complaints and questions we hear regarding Millennials:

- How can I get them to be loyal?

- Do we need to shift our entire workplace culture to coddle younger team members?

- Trying to get them to work overtime is like pulling teeth.

- They are too sensitive to confrontation.

- Why can't I just get them to do what I want them to do?

- They don't listen to what I say.

- Where can I find people who don't need to be coddled?

If you're a Boomer or Gen Xer who shares these concerns about Millennials, remember they have a list of concerns about you as well. I suggest you take the time to understand how they think instead of allowing your frustrations to guide you. A recent Gallup poll revealed that 71% of Millennials are either not engaged or actively *disengaged* at work.[13] Furthermore, six in 10 millennials say they're open to different job opportunities, and only 50% plan to be with their current company in 12 months.

It may also be worth considering a study by Universum Global stating that Gen Xers, Millennials, and Gen Zers actually share similar concerns:

- Becoming a leader is important to the majority of each of the three generations (57% Gen X, 61% Gen Y, 61% Gen Z).

- About half of them worry whether their personalities fit in where they work (40% Gen X, 50% Gen Y, 50% Gen Z).

- All three generations are concerned about their stress levels and work-life balance.

What should you do? Take the time to talk to them about what's important to them personally. Get to know what motivates them, identify their generational tendencies, and look for opportunities to inspire and encourage. Michael Dimock, Pew Research Center's president, put it well when he said, "[Keep] in mind that generations

---

13 https://news.gallup.com/businessjournal/195209/few-millennials-engaged-work.aspx

are a lens through which to understand societal change, rather than a label with which to oversimplify differences between groups."[14]

A Cultural Shift Is Underway

For the first time in history, there are five generations in the workforce at the same time. However, for the first time in almost 60 years, the participation of retirees (those 65 and older) in the workforce has cracked the 20 percent mark. "Unretirement" is becoming more common. A 2010 study by Nicole Maestas,[15] an economist at Harvard Medical School, reveals that more than 25% of retirees go back to work after saying they've retired. A more recent 2017 study from RAND Corporation[16] revealed that 40% of workers over 65 had previously retired.

Labor Force Share, by Age Group, 1998, 2008, 2018, and Projected 2028

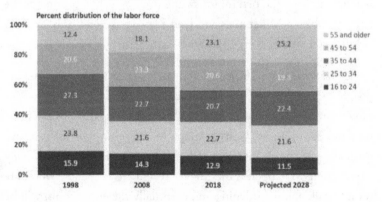

14 http://www.pewresearch.org/fact-tank/2018/03/01/defining-generations-where-millennials-end-and-post-millennials-begin/?amp=1
15 https://www.ncbi.nlm.nih.gov/pmc/articles/PMC4004604/
16 https://www.rand.org/pubs/research_reports/RR2014.html

By 2028, a little more than 25% of the workforce is projected to be over the age of 55[17] compared to only about 12% of the workforce in 1994. This diversity can certainly provide benefits in terms of the unique backgrounds and perspectives that each generation brings. It can also lead to misunderstandings and conflict. Recognizing the potential for conflict and taking steps to proactively minimize that potential can help ensure a high-functioning and positive culture—one in which multiple perspectives from different generations can thrive.

According to the US Census Bureau, Millennials and Gen Zers now outnumber Baby Boomers in the workforce. Gen Xers, however, won't surpass Boomers in the workforce until 2028. Why is that?

Baby Boomers didn't have as many children as previous generations due to the recession in the late 1970s and early 1980s. There was even a term given to this phenomenon: DINK, which stands for "dual income, no kids." Once their children, the Gen Xers, started having children, the pendulum swung back, which accounts for the large number of Millennials and Gen Zers. In the end, this creates a culture shift that becomes a numbers game.

Let's say there are 20 people at a party. Then I bring in 10 more people to mingle with the other guests, but these 10 people specifically want to talk about gardening. What do you think will happen in about 30 minutes? Conversations in the room will shift toward gardening. If the people who talk about gardening stay, eventually what's going to happen is that the party will attract people who only want to talk about gardening and eventually the entire room will be

---

17 https://www.bls.gov/opub/mlr/2015/article/labor-force-projections-to-2024.htm; https://www.bls.gov/emp/images/lf_aging.png

talking about it. It doesn't matter what the topic may be—the same goes for sports, movies, or cooking.

The point is that when you introduce a large group of like-minded people, they are going to change the conversation. On a much bigger scale, it impacts the culture.

Think about how business owners and managers for many years fostered independence, long hours, rigid structure, and hard work as a way to grow their companies. Millennials (and I believe Gen Zers) are not content to lead in the same manner.

A study by American Express asked Millennials whether or not they aspire to executive roles in the same manner as previous generations.[18] While seven in 10 respondents said they aspire to become C-Suite executives, more than a third said they don't believe in that kind of hierarchy. Furthermore, while 91% of Millennials said they aspire to leadership roles, 83% would prefer to work for companies with fewer layers of management.[19]

As those individuals enter into business and impact the culture, they will redefine leadership. Instead of being detached and focusing on a top-down approach, future CEOs will promote collaboration and support harmony, balance, integrity, and teamwork.

Generational diversity can work to a company's competitive advantage. Experience and youth can be a powerful combination that leads to creativity and innovation. But that same diversity can be a company's greatest weakness if people within the organization are stubborn and unwilling to collaborate, compromise, or understand the strengths and weaknesses of a different generation.

---

18 https://www.businessnewsdaily.com/10507-millennial-leadership-executive-tips.html
19 https://workplacetrends.com/the-millennial-leadership-survey/

It sounds daunting, but it doesn't have to be. All impactful change starts at the top with leadership, and it begins with everyone getting on the same page. When you bring an entire company together and train your people properly, generational boundaries disintegrate and people begin to collaborate.

What We Do at RedRock Leadership

When I first walked into the office of J-TEK International, it felt more like I was walking on to the set of *Boiler Room* or *Glengarry Glen Ross*. The executives were upstairs, and the sales team was downstairs. The whole layout was a throwback to the 1980s and 1990s, which made sense after I met Craig, the owner. His office was on the first floor, which was dark, cluttered, and disorganized. The place had a "survival of the fittest" feel.

When I sat down with Craig, he told me how the company had been in business for more than 30 years, but sales were flat and he couldn't get the company to grow. He told me it felt like he was stuck doing everything by himself. It was clear that he wasn't very happy with his team—a team he assembled. He was upset he was spending so much money on his team and not seeing results.

I wasn't sitting across from him for more than five minutes before I could tell he was a guy who needed to be in control and didn't trust very easily. He certainly didn't trust me. He mentioned that he had seen the positive reviews RedRock Leadership had received on Google but seemed reluctant to believe them.

It turned out that the company was actually founded by Craig's grandfather, who handed it down to Craig's dad, who then expected

Craig to take over where he left off. Craig watched his grandfather and his dad go at it for years. His grandfather hoarded money, and his dad always wanted to spend it. He described his dad as a very proud man who thought he knew the best way to run the business. I could tell Craig had his doubts about the way his dad did things. Not only did Craig not want me to meet his dad, he didn't even want his dad to know he was bringing me in. But his back was up against the wall, and he was running out of ideas and options for getting the business to grow. It was like Craig was expecting someone to show up and be the ghostwriter of his success.

Craig walked me around to meet the team. His sales manager, Monica, was a lot like Craig. She seemed cautious, somewhat skeptical, and very reluctant to have me there. It was obvious to me that she believed my presence meant she wasn't doing her job. She kept referring to the training she received when she was a retail sales manager 25 years ago. In all of this, I was imagining Craig running from his father and Monica running from Craig.

Next, I met the most senior sales rep, Charles. He was the epitome of the throwback salesman, right down to the hardback leather briefcase. He was the grizzled "seen it all and just want to go out there and sell" type. He didn't give a hoot about anyone else, and this attitude was working for him because he was the only one who was accomplishing his sales goals.

When I met him, he appeared to be going with the flow. Little did I know he had his own gripes, but for the time being, he appeared to be on board with Craig and Monica. It wasn't the most productive first meeting, but Craig invited me back to meet the rest of the team and give them a sample of my training. That's when things started to make more sense.

The sales team was an eclectic group, from young people with very little experience all the way up to team members like Charles, who seemed to have an endless number of war stories. Almost immediately after I got started, I got massive pushback from a few members of the team. I was caught off guard. I was presenting information about how to trust, persevere, and collaborate—but I was witnessing the exact opposite play out in front of me in real time. There were a few people, however, who seemed to soak up everything I said. They were actually on board with the training and were attentive and willing to learn.

The more I talked, the more I got the impression something wasn't right, so I shifted gears and convinced Craig and Monica to leave the room so that I could be alone with the sales team. That's when Charles came out of his shell and made it clear that he didn't see any value whatsoever in me being there.

"What are you doing here? We're not the problem! We don't need any of this!" he shouted. "Craig is clueless, and Monica doesn't do anything. She lets Craig run the show and does whatever he says."

It turned out Charles came to the company to work for Craig's dad and was frustrated watching (as he saw it) Craig destroy what his father and grandfather built. Charles told me the entire company was a train wreck.

Everyone started opening up, and they told me how the company had been through a massive amount of change over the past three years. There had been a lot of turnover on the operations team, and it seemed like there was a revolving door of people coming and going in the sales department. The company's culture was unrecognizable. It was a free-for-all. It became clear to me that the team wasn't the problem, Craig was the problem.

I knew it was going to be much more challenging than I had first thought, and I began to wonder if I'd bitten off more than I could chew.

CHAPTER 2

CAN'T WE JUST ELIMINATE EMOTIONS?

To understand what was happening at Craig's company, it's important to talk about emotions. Emotions are powerful!

They can be the fuel that motivates you, and they can also be the debilitating force that brings your productivity to a grinding halt, jeopardizing important personal and business relationships.

This makes me think of a quote by John Kotter, a professor of leadership at Harvard Business School and an internationally known speaker on business, leadership, and change.

"Because of the furious pace of change in business today, difficult-to-manage relationships sabotage more business than anything else," he said. "It's not a question of strategy that gets us into trouble, it's a question of emotions."

Let me ask you a true-or-false question that I typically ask participants during RedRock Leadership training: To manage the furious pace of change today, humans can and sometimes need to eliminate emotions before making critical decisions. Is this true or false?

More often than not, the room is a 50/50 split. Some people get it while others insist it's true and yell out something like, "When you fire someone, you must remove your emotions so you can make that tough decision." But that's a flawed thought process. Even if we want to eliminate our emotions, it doesn't mean we can. This is because our brains actually use and interpret our emotions so that we can respond to external stimuli with rational behavior.[20] In other words, it's impossible for us to put aside emotions when making decisions because emotions are an innate part of our decision-making process.

The research findings of Antonio Damasio, University of Southern California professor of psychology, philosophy, and neurology, describe how emotions guide behavior and decision-making and play a central role in social cognition. In his 1994 book, *Descartes' Error: Emotion, Reason and the Human Brain*, Damasio argues that René Descartes's "error" was his belief in the separation of mind and body, rationality and emotion.

Damasio also gives an account of one of his patients, referred to as "Elliott," who had a brain tumor removed from the frontal lobe of his brain. Prior to the tumor, he had a good job, was a role model to his younger siblings, and was a good husband. However, after the tumor was removed, his decision-making was hindered because his brain could no longer process his emotions.

Damasio describes Elliott's dilemma this way: "Try to imagine not feeling pleasure when you contemplate a painting you love or hear a favorite piece of music. Try to imagine yourself forever robbed of that possibility and yet aware of the intellectual contents of the visual or musical stimulus, and also aware that once it did give

---

20 https://www.technologyreview.com/s/528151/the-importance-of-feelings/; https://www.nature.com/articles/nrn3403

you pleasure. We might summarize Elliot's predicament as to know but not to feel."

Damasio and other brain researchers have shown how our emotions guide our actions. This translates powerfully to the business world, where we must learn to leverage our emotions so we can make on-time critical decisions and give our organizations a creative and competitive advantage.

It All Comes Down to Trust

The problem at J-TEK International might have seemed overwhelming to me at first, but it wasn't a unique problem. I've seen similar problems in organizations that specialize in marketing, transportation, contracting, distribution, IT, manufacturing, construction, and insurance, to name a few. Craig could be Steve, Jon, Donald, Sarah, Jessica, or any number of the business owners with whom I've worked. On the surface, these businesses and their owners may look different, but when you peel back the onion, you can see that they share the common goal of wanting to control their people and their surrounding environment.

How can we fix that? It certainly doesn't happen overnight. So much of what I do when it comes to working with people in leadership comes down to trust. I can relate because I tend to be a distrustful person myself. People who don't trust will face significant challenges. When you don't trust your team, they won't follow you. It's a vicious cycle.

What is trust? When I ask this question during a RedRock Leadership training session, responses are all over the map. It's an interesting and complex question, for sure. Here are the answers that seem to make the most sense to me:[21]

1. Trust is an action guided by an emotion.

2. Trust is an emotion that triggers an action.

3. Trust is a feeling of security, a sense that someone cares about our well-being.

4. Trust is part of complex neural processes of which we are not always conscious.

I have worked with and coached thousands of people from all different walks of life. I may not have the depth of knowledge of a neuroscientist, philosopher, or psychologist, but I do believe I'm qualified to conclude that trust is a central part of all interpersonal relationships. I want to encourage you to be aware of your thinking and behavior when it comes to trust so it doesn't hinder your ability to make decisions and take risks.

Once you understand your willingness and ability to trust and how it impacts your thoughts and actions, you'll become a stronger person. You'll begin to notice it makes sense to manage your emotions and let them guide you into action, rather than the other way around. This is when you'll realize that fear—of not getting what you want or losing something you have—is the root cause of your inability to trust and it's holding you back from trusting your people and processes.

If you are someone who has a "when I feel they trust me, I'll trust them" mentality, you'll lack the ability to be collaborative. If you want others to trust you, you must first trust them. Leading

---

21 https://www.psychologytoday.com/us/blog/hot-thought/201810/what-is-trust

by example is always the most effective form of leadership. Also, remember choosing to trust doesn't need to be all or nothing. As a business owner, I don't need to trust my team with my deepest thoughts or with my children, but I need to trust them to hit their numbers or complete a project on time.

For me to put Kevin into that ballgame, I needed to trust that he learned what I taught him. If I let my emotions own me, I would have kept him out of the game out of fear he would make an error and make me look bad as a coach. I learned this the hard way. I've had far too many instances where I caught myself thinking or even saying something like, "When Kevin shows me he has the level of confidence he needs to be on that ballfield, I'll put him in the game." It was the other way around. I had to trust that he was ready, regardless of whether or not he looked confident out on the field.

Those who enter a conversation on the assumption that it will be a positive interaction and who are committed to trust will promote collaboration. If we instill in our teams that it all comes down to trust, we have to trust them first if we expect them to respond positively and trust us in return.

Identify the Best and Worst Leaders That You Have Encountered in Your Life

Take a minute and write down the best leader you've ever encountered and describe that person's traits and reputation. Next, think of the worst leader you've ever encountered and describe that person's traits and reputation. Once you finish, think about the impact that each of those individuals has had on your life.

For me, the answer to these questions is easy. By far, the best leader I ever encountered was a guy named Tom and the worst was a guy named Terry. They were polar opposites, but I learned important lessons from both of them.

Tom cared. He listened to what I had to say. He was patient and exercised tough love. He wasn't just a "yes" man and he wasn't afraid to confront me. Even when he was stern, I could tell that he cared about my well-being. When I was 20 years old and working at Tom's company, I was irresponsible and did something that offended someone in the office. Tom pulled me aside and got me in line. He helped me understand I was putting myself in a bad situation by acting in a way I shouldn't. I respected him for that and I never forgot it. I felt like he was investing in my future success and that he was interested in me as a person.

When it was time for me to move on, I went to work for another company where Terry was my manager, and there couldn't have been more of a contrast. Terry was extremely critical, abrasive, and genuinely uncaring. If I gave him my sales report on Thursday, it would be back on my desk by Friday with harsh critiques scrawled in red ink. Never did any of those remarks come with explanations. I don't recall him ever using my name when we spoke, and he never looked me in the eye. It felt like Terry was someone who cared more about himself than the people he led.

The impact these two men had on me was significant. Whenever I talk to people about leadership, I always think back to the way Tom invested in and cared for his team. I find that I have the best results when I take a page from Tom's book and do it in a way that helps someone grow and learn.

There have been times throughout my career when I've noticed elements of Terry pop up in me as well. It has taken me years to finally realize Terry didn't know how to be a leader because he was reluctant to trust others and didn't take the time to manage his emotions. He wasn't ready to be a successful manager. I often wonder if he ever wanted to be in that position at all. When I'm in a difficult situation, I do my best to deal with my insecurities and manage my emotions so that I can assume positive intent, establish trust, and then take action.

Lead with Emotional Intelligence

Emotional intelligence is a term used by many, while very few people actually know what it means and even fewer know its origin. It's been traced back to the early 1900s. However, it wasn't until the 1960s when Orval Mowrer, an American psychologist and professor of psychology at the University of Illinois, put forth the idea that emotions exist on a spectrum.

The term "emotional intelligence" first appeared in 1964 in a paper written by Michael Beldoch, a psychologist at Cornell University. This paper was followed by a doctoral thesis written by Wayne Leon Payne in 1985 called, "A Study of Emotion: Developing Emotional Intelligence."

Soon after, in 1990, psychologists Peter Salovey and John Mayer published an article defining emotional intelligence as the subset of social intelligence that involves the ability to monitor one's own and others' feelings and emotions, to discriminate among them, and to use this information to guide one's thinking and actions. In the article, they also presented a framework for the concept of emotional intelligence.

Daniel Goleman, a science journalist for the *New York Times*, popularized the term "emotional intelligence" in 1995 with his book, *Emotional Intelligence: Why It Can Matter More than IQ.*

RedRock Leadership recognizes emotional intelligence as one's ability to manage individual emotions as well as the emotions of others while making critical decisions, trusting others, and persevering through difficult to manage situations. Emotional intelligence is measured by emotional quotient (EQ) and should not be confused with intelligence quotient (IQ), which is a measure of one's cognitive ability to recognize patterns and solve problems.

EQ is massively more important than IQ when it comes to identifying and developing leaders.[22] This is because, now more than ever, those in leadership positions are required to quickly assess positive and negative situations and keep team engagement levels high.

RedRock Leadership focuses on these five key skills that will help you improve EQ in yourself and others:

1. **Personal Awareness:** Your ability to recognize your influence on others.

2. **Integrity:** Your ability to match your intentions to your actions.

3. **Internal Motivation:** Your ability to do the right things for the right reasons.

---

22 https://www.inc.com/steve-goldstein/eq-is-massively-more-important-than-iq-for-leaders-heres-why.html

4.   **Empathy:** Your ability to recognize and share the emotions of others.

5.   **Social Skills:** Your ability to build positive relationships.

(If you are interested in knowing your EQ, visit RedRockLeadership.com/the-book for details about the TTI Success Insights˚ assessment tool that measures your emotional intelligence through an online questionnaire that is immediately analyzed to produce a detailed report. There is also information there about how to become certified in EQ.)

These five skills can be separated into two main skill sets:

- **Intrapersonal Skills:** These are the internal skills. Personal awareness, integrity, and internal motivation are developed and strengthened on the inside.

- **Interpersonal Skills:** These skills include empathy and social skills and relate to relationships and situations between two or more people.

We all know people who lack empathy and social skills—perhaps you know them as narcissists. They tend to think and talk only about themselves. When you come in contact with these people, be careful not to jump to the conclusion that they're bad people or have bad intentions. In many cases, they think they're personally aware but they're not.

Personal awareness is in unusually short supply in today's workplace. A nearly five-year study conducted by *Harvard Business Review*[23] discovered that although 95% of people think they're personally aware, only 10%–15% actually are. In many cases, people

---

23 https://hbr.org/2018/10/working-with-people-who-arent-self-aware

may think they're responding in a less selfish way but they aren't. Before you can respond to others, you need to be aware of yourself.

Developing intrapersonal skills such as self-esteem and open-mindedness can be challenging because we are all wired differently. This is especially true for those who are critical, non-trusting, and self-dependent, even more so if they're expected to lead others. These types of people tend to get a lot of push back from those who don't deal well with confrontation.

Each of us has stress and insecurities that hinder interpersonal communication, and until we deal with them, we'll continue to struggle in our relationships with others. To improve our interpersonal skills, we must first improve our intrapersonal skills, which is ultimately how we will become more emotionally intelligent.

The Three Levels of Emotional Intelligence

As we improve our intrapersonal skill sets, our interpersonal skills improve, raising our EQ. However, we can expect that our EQ will always fluctuate based on what's going on in and around us.

During RedRock Leadership training, we illustrate this fluctuation by identifying three individual personas, or attitude types. Let me introduce you to Laggards, Loners, and Leaders.

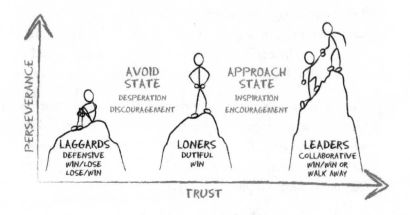

Laggards: Laggards are defensive. They tend to let other people and external factors define their identity. They view life through an "I win/you lose," "I lose/you win," or "I lose/you lose" paradigm, or mental filter. They don't persevere nor do they trust people and processes. In fact, they rarely trust themselves.

Laggards feel sorry for themselves and want others to feel sorry for them. They continuously fall behind. They're desperate and discouraged. Because of this mentality, they can draw others into their way of thinking and cause them to feel desperate and discouraged too.

It's not unusual for laggards to be unaware of their detrimental state of mind until someone helps them understand. It may take drastic circumstances for them to come to grips with it, but once someone is able to identify and admit they're behaving like a laggard, they can change. However, the longer someone is a laggard, the more challenging it can be for he or she to develop the five key skills of emotional intelligence.

Loners: Loners are dutiful. They persevere just enough to get what they want. They tend to exist in a silo, and they view what's going on around them through an "I win" paradigm. Loners are great at getting things done and making money, but they're not so good at creating a legacy. The favorite one-liner of a loner is, "I've got this."

I don't want to overlook the idea that sometimes it's necessary to get into a silo to block out all the noise going on around us and get things done. However, if we're unconsciously existing as a loner, it can cause big problems because we tend to stop listening and start overcommunicating our point just to get our way.

It can be easy to enable the negative tendencies of loners who are productive. The fact that they don't "play nice in the sandbox" or tend to be bossy and self-centered may cause us to overlook the way they behave because of their high level of productivity and ability to generate profit. A loner can be desperate and discouraging one day, only to be inspiring and encouraging the next. The long-term effects of behaving like a loner are detrimental to the relationships around them.

Leaders: Leaders are collaborative. They trust others and they trust the process. They've learned how to persevere in the face of adversity. They live life through an "I win/you win or I walk away" paradigm.

RedRock Leadership training gets people to a place where they can exist at this level for extended periods of time. Leaders are not only encouraged and inspired but they encourage and inspire others.

Leaders have mental toughness and know how to sustain it. They are straightforward, honest, and assertive communicators. They know how to create win-win relationships. They are exceptional at conflict resolution and negotiation. They have an abundance mentality. Leaders persevere through disappointments and setbacks and power through tough times. They are exceptional at managing their emotions and know how to walk away before a situation becomes unmanageable.

Leaders have healthy habits. They are mentors and coaches who bring the best out in others. Leaders guide others to a positive future. A willingness to trust people and processes while persevering through difficult situations raises EQ and positively impacts the ability to lead.

I really believe that a leader's ultimate goal is to create a legacy, one that reflects how well they cared for and took care of others.

Management vs. Leadership

Let me make something very clear—something that you may have already realized. It's possible to occupy a position in "leadership" and not be a leader. Conversely, it's possible to be leader and not be considered part of "leadership."

So how do you define leadership?

That question stumped me for a long time. Back in 2009, one year before I started RedRock Leadership, I did a ton of research on the subject because I couldn't get my mind around it. I heard all kinds of definitions. One person said to me, "Leadership is defined by who's behind you. If nobody is following you, then you aren't a leader." Well, that didn't help me. Someone else said, "To understand leadership, you need to understand if it's taught or caught." That didn't help me either.

As I dug deeper into the topic of leadership, I began to realize it was easier for me to define leadership by first looking at what leadership is not. It became clear that much of what people defined as leadership was actually management and the two are very different.

My conclusion? Management is tactical and leadership is conceptual.

"Do as I say and not as I do" is a well-known phrase and one that previous generations leaned on heavily. Traditionalists said, "Management tells me what to do," and Baby Boomers looked at management and said, "Really I know best." Then along came the Gen Xers who said, "We need a hero." Perhaps, this is what led to the idea that we need managers to oversee the work of others. Today, our culture is shifting, and we've reached a point where we're encouraged to do a lot of independent thinking, even if it challenges management.

Personally, I think management is an overrated, outdated, and overstated discipline. Why do I believe this? Well, for starters, some of the best authors of "management" books are no longer with us. Very few people are even writing about the topic anymore. Too many business owners and executives think they lead their organization when what they really do is manage or, in the case of many with whom I come in contact, they micromanage.

Craig at J-TEK International fell into this category. He didn't understand why he couldn't scale the business, which had been around for many years. He had quality products, great service, and the company was profitable. He came up through the family business as a salesman, and he was a really good one. He was a competitive problem-solver with a knack for warming up to people quickly; as soon as he was in charge, he made sure he was calling all of the shots. It got to the point where he undermined everything Monica did. She seemed incredibly qualified but it was Craig's show. It's not uncommon for business owners like Craig to create chaotic energy without even realizing it. Their lack of trust in others tends to create tension and lead others to question their motives.

When things got tough, Craig got tougher. His competitive juices began to flow. He started off by having meetings with his staff to tighten rules and ensure that they would work full days and do what he thought they needed to do to be successful. Next, he revamped the sales team's compensation plan—again. He thought if he added rewards for hitting quotas and penalties for missing them that the team would sell more and perform better. When he still didn't get the results he wanted, he called another meeting and put pressure on the team by reminding them of the consequences for not following the systems and processes he put in place.

Nothing worked, and as a last resort, Craig installed time clocks for all members of his team. He demanded weekly sales reports from the sales team but never seemed satisfied with what they gave him, so he rearranged the cubicles and offices to have a better view of what they were doing. He even put cameras on the sales floor to see what was going on from his office. After growing frustrated when he couldn't hear what was being said, he installed devices on every team member's computer so he could watch their screens from the quad-screen monitor in his office.

Two months into working with Craig, I got a call from him.

"Jeff, I think you should know what's going on. I'm staring at Charles' monitor right now, and he's erased and rewritten the same email five times," he said. "I think he needs you to help him write an email."

I couldn't believe what I was hearing. This is really bad. Is this even legal? What's so interesting is that behavior like this isn't uncommon. I worked with another business owner who put GPS devices on all of his outside salespeople's cars so he could see where they went during the day. I bet more than five out of every 10 small business owners have gone to this length. The problem is that a manager operating with a low EQ (at the laggard or loner level) will ultimately become a micromanager, looking over everyone's shoulders and judging every little thing they do.

If this style of management-driven leadership doesn't work today, what does?

The Rise of Collaborative Leadership

As the chairman and CEO of General Electric for two decades, Jack Welch grew revenue from $25 billion to $130 billion and profit from $1.5 billion to $15 billion. His aggressive style made him a hero to many Baby Boomers and up-and-coming Gen Xers. He was a dominant figure in business leadership and management. He believed that managers should fire the bottom 10 percent of their workforce every year to increase profit and the stock price along with it. His executive team had faith in him and seemed willing to follow him down any path.

Jack Welch influenced his followers through a top-down style of leadership. This is an approach where the person in charge defines and communicates the strategy, assigns roles, motivates followers, evaluates execution, stack ranks them, and then rewards performers and eliminates non-performers.

There are still several people today who subscribe to this outdated leadership model, but it's becoming increasingly more obvious that people aren't going to tolerate those who force their personal agendas by calling all the shots. People don't want to work for someone who rules the company from on high. Rather, they want to be part of a collaborative work environment. They want to be led by someone who operates with purpose and cares about them and the organization. They want to be trusted, and they want to be part of something bigger than themselves.

I'm continuing to see that success depends less on the heroic actions of a few individuals at the top and more on interdependent, collaborative leadership practices distributed throughout an organization. Today, people are not looking for a career as much as they're looking for an experience. They value flexibility and free time, and they want to feel as though they're working toward accomplishing goals together. This goes against the grain of those people in charge who want to create a highly competitive workplace. It's important to know that today's workforce wants to be part of something great, something with purpose. If you push or lead them the wrong way, expect that eventually they'll leave your organization for greener pastures.

This shift in culture may seem sudden and jarring to some, but many have seen the writing on the wall for a while now. As early as 2001, in his book *Good to Great,* author and consultant Jim Collins wrote about "good" being the enemy of "great." He calls out five levels of leadership, stating that most reside at level four, where their leadership abilities are considered good. He goes on to explain that great leaders reside at level five. What's most interesting is how closely level four and level five leadership styles resemble the heroic and collaborative leadership styles of today.

Here are six differences between collaborative leadership and heroic leadership:

1. Trust Is an Action vs. Trust Is an Emotion

We've already talked about trust. A signature trait of highly collaborative people is that they view trust as an action that's guided by their emotions as opposed to those who view trust more like an emotion that triggers their actions. As I mentioned earlier, many people I work with who are in charge admit that they don't trust anyone. I get the same reaction every time I suggest they trust others: "You've got to be kidding me!"

For those of you who grew up in or around the sales profession, you've probably heard the phrase, "Buyers are liars." This was part of my training as a young salesman. I'm not saying that some buyers aren't liars but today most buyers trust the online ratings of others. Remember that the core behaviors of Gen Zers are all anchored in one element, their search for truth. Trust begets confidence, so if you're not assuming positive intent from the outset, you're setting yourself back.

2. Coach vs. Criticize

Heroic leadership calls for constructive criticism and confrontation, while collaborative leadership focuses on coaching. Don't roll your eyes. It's coaching and not coddling. There's a big difference and this isn't a new idea either.

In his book, *How to Win Friends and Influence People*, Dale Carnegie writes that it's easy to "criticize, condemn, and complain" but that it takes "character and self-control to be understanding."

And he tells this story about a man named Bob Hoover to make his point:

"Bob Hoover, a famous test pilot and frequent performer at air shows, was returning to his home in Los Angeles from an air show in San Diego. As described in the magazine, *Flight Operations*, at 300 feet in the air, both engines suddenly stopped. With deft maneuvering, he managed to land and no one was hurt, but the plane was badly damaged. Hoover's first act after the emergency landing was to inspect the airplane's fuel. Just as he suspected, his World War II propeller plane was filled with jet fuel rather than gasoline.

Upon returning to the airport, he asked to see the mechanic who had serviced his airplane. The young man was sick with the agony of his mistake. Tears streamed down his face as Hoover approached. He had just caused the loss of a very expensive plane and could have caused the loss of three lives as well. You can imagine Hoover's anger. One could anticipate the tongue-lashing that this proud and precise pilot would unleash for that carelessness. But Hoover didn't scold the mechanic; he didn't even criticize him. Instead, he put his big arm around the man's shoulder and said, 'To show you I'm sure that you'll never do this again, I want you to service my F-51 tomorrow.'"

Those people who are aligned with collaborative leadership practices prepare their minds and modify their actions, and they are therefore seen in a positive light by others. This approach ultimately improves the level of emotional intelligence throughout an entire organization.

3. Trust Gut Instinct vs. Rely on Core Values

Heroic leadership is a practice that says it's acceptable to hire and fire people based on a gut instinct, while those aligned with the principles of collaborative leadership make decisions to hire and fire based on an individual's adherence to the organization's core values. How many times have you leaned on your own personal bias and said, "I just have a good feeling about this person" or "I just feel this person isn't going to turn the corner?" I've heard it said that if you trust your gut, you'll be right 65 percent of the time. What few people seem to realize is that it also means you'll be wrong 35 percent of the time. In order to follow the principles of collaborative leadership, you must set aside your own personal bias and let your core values guide your decision-making process.

4. Credit Others vs. Take Credit

Those people who exhibit a heroic style of leadership take credit for the positive results that happen on their watch, while those who are more collaborative credit their teams for their well-earned success. The latter approach goes far in developing trust and getting others to trust you. Let's face it, heroes are in it for themselves. The fact is that they're not leaders at all but counterfeit leaders who create a toxic and cutthroat culture. Acknowledging the members of your team gives them the opportunity to feel like they're part of something positive and good—something bigger than themselves. This type of culture is healthy and will promote long-term growth and stability.

5. Accept Responsibility vs. Blame Others

Those confined to a heroic style of leadership blame their teams for poor results, while those who are collaborative accept responsibility when things don't go as planned. This is a two-way street. Highly collaborative people are true leaders who understand they must take the good with the bad. The trust you earn by giving your team credit for their victories goes right out the window if you place blame on them for defeats. Don't get me wrong—this doesn't mean that you don't hold your team accountable. It means that you win with the team and you lose with the team. If you adhere to the principles of collaborative leadership, you shoulder the brunt of the blame and accept responsibility in order for your team to have the confidence and freedom to take risks.

6. Serve Others vs. Take Control

If you are someone who is adamant about having to be in control to protect your reputation, you're adhering to a heroic style of leadership. As you become more emotionally intelligent, you'll become more collaborative and your focus will shift from controlling to caring.

I admit, I'm a recovering control freak, and most business owners or people in leadership positions have taken control of their lives and careers. If you're someone who fears failure, it's natural to build the walls higher while your arms grow longer so you can keep everything under your control. We do this to protect our reputations. But the more I let go and trust others, the faster and stronger the growth.

As you become more collaborative, you will become someone who is very good at assembling a team and then showing them you trust them by giving them the freedom to operate. This requires coaching and promoting the people you know you can count on, as well as harnessing the harmful behavior of the ones who are not a match for the culture. This means making sure everyone is on the same page and working toward a common goal. In the end, a collaborative team is always stronger than the individual heroes.

None of these changes will happen overnight. No business owner can realistically shift gears and suddenly turn his or her back on a style that has been ingrained in them for years. It takes time, and the first step is changing the way you think—and more specifically, the way you act.

The Approach State vs. the Avoid State

In challenging situations, when critical decisions and sensible choices are necessary, an increased level of emotional intelligence is imperative to gain trust and develop a loyal following.

To raise EQ, we must have a mindset congruent with growth. That mindset is called the "Approach State." It's in direct contrast to the "Avoid State" mindset that demonstrates low EQ and is a hindrance to growth. When you're in the Approach State, others feel comfortable approaching you and you approach difficult-to-manage situations with determination and confidence. When you're in the Avoid State, others tend to avoid you and you avoid difficult-to-manage situations.

APPROACH STATE	AVOID STATE
Inspired by the success of others	Threatened by the success of others
Looks at the big picture and seeks a solution	Demotivated by obstacles
Learns from coaching	Ignores useful feedback
Coaches others	Criticizes others
Overcomes adversity	Gives up easily

Laggards stay in the Avoid State while leaders thrive in the Approach State. This isn't always a conscious choice but it needs to be one. There are very few people who wake up with a desire to live in the Avoid State, yet many people do. If you're stuck in that rut, it takes a conscious effort to pull yourself out of it, but first you must realize you can choose how you want to behave. The Approach State and Avoid State are not mindsets forced upon us; they are mindsets we must choose.

Once you train yourself to stay in the Approach State, your way of thinking and being will influence others. I lead a Bible study and watched this way of thinking spread among my group of ninth grade students. One day, one of them said to me, "Hey, Mr. Jeff, we're thinking about getting together on Tuesday nights to hold ourselves accountable."

They made a list of all the things they wanted to discuss and for which they wanted to be held accountable. I was blown away. It was clear to me that they were committed to developing a stronger faith.

"Wow, guys, this is great," I said. "I don't think I can make it on Tuesday night. Is there another night that will work instead?"

"Oh no, Mr. Jeff. We don't want you there."

I had to laugh because, naturally, I thought that I had to control the process. Instead, I needed to step back and trust them while letting them know I would be there as a guide if they needed me. Talk about amazing. Imagine if your team said that they were getting together to talk and hold themselves accountable to make sure everyone was doing the right thing. And they were doing it on their own, without you! Wouldn't that be an unbelievable feeling?

That isn't a far-fetched scenario. It happens when you operate from the Approach State and trust your team to execute their own ideas. This is how they will find their own way to accountability.

I recognize this when I work with sales teams. Any time I put specific rules on anything—start times, finish times, quotas, or any kind of cap—the team always seems to work right up to that finish time or quota and then stop. But if I remove the cap and don't give them any specific rules, the team will work longer hours and do more than I expected. It's similar to the way a negotiation with a customer unfolds; if you let the customer go first, they will almost always agree to pay more than you would have offered.

To drive this point home during RedRock Leadership training, I hold up a mason jar with a perforated lid and tell the following story:

"Imagine me putting a flea in this jar, then tightening its perforated lid. The flea would jump around, trying with all its might to escape the jar. Then after a day or so, when I remove the lid, the flea will finally escape, right? Actually, it won't. It's an interesting phenomenon that the flea will actually learn to accept its limits and won't know how to move past them, even when the physical barrier is literally lifted away."

As interesting as that may be, it leads us to a rather unwelcome comparison. We aren't much different from fleas in this regard. Perceived limits will do nothing but strike us down and keep us from achieving our desired results until our efforts slowly trickle to a halt. Then if our circumstances do change, we're used to being stuck and we fail to see new opportunities, just like the flea.

We aren't fleas and we aren't physically trapped without hope of escape. We can and should work at overcoming limitations—especially self-imposed limitations.

In the Approach State, we are encouraged and inspired without limits. This is when we are at our best and we persevere while trusting others as well as our systems and processes. In contrast, we are discouraged and desperate in the Avoid State. Where there are no limits, we create them by imposing rules and quotas to make up for a lack of trust.

Those who operate as leaders have a high EQ and maintain a prolonged existence in the Approach State. Laggards and unconscious loners have a low-level EQ and maintain a prolonged existence in the Avoid State.

Those who have yet to develop and hone their emotional intelligence skills will live much of their lives in the Avoid State. They strive to be heroes and they haven't developed the skills to be collaborative. That's why they panic when their companies hit a wall and they don't experience the growth they think they should.

The Dangers of the Avoid State

I hate traffic! It's one of those things in life that, if I'm not careful, will land me smack dab in the center of the Avoid State. Living in Tampa has forever conditioned me to despise it. When I'm in other cities, I can't believe it when it takes me only 20 minutes to get to the airport when the same trip in Tampa would take me an hour. Regardless of your stressors, those unpleasant experiences are a sure-fire way to move you into the Avoid State. Even when I don't have a place to go, I get stressed out by traffic—something my wife points out frequently. Why does that happen?

We are conditioned by our past experiences. Most of us have experienced financial stress and relationship trauma, so when you enter a situation that feels familiar in that way, your body responds by secreting the stress hormones adrenaline and cortisol.

In moderate levels, stress can be healthy and lead to creativity, but when it's too high, or builds up over time, that increased cortisol and adrenaline can actually cause your body to break down. That makes it difficult to get ourselves out of even moderately stressful situations. Adrenaline, blood pressure, heart rate, and blood sugar levels all increase. This can lead to shakiness, muscle tension, dilated pupils, ulcers, and the release of epinephrine into our blood stream which can disrupt digestion and immune system function.

When we're under consistent, underlying stress, what used to be considered a normal level of cortisol is elevated to a point where our bodies become desensitized and our creativity is hindered. If you can keep your cortisol levels low, while getting adequate sleep so your body produces healthy growth hormones, the positive effects are bountiful: creativity increases, heart rate and blood sugar level decrease, your muscles relax, digestion and immune function improve, you become more stable, and consequently your EQ will rise.

You're limited when you reside in the Avoid State and that lessens your influence, which is why it's so important to pay attention to your stressors and your mindset. However, that can be easier said than done since we're all human. Nobody sets out to be stressed, so during those vulnerable moments when stress happens, we find ourselves in the Avoid State without even realizing it.

It helps to anticipate your stressors and look to what energizes you. What in your life has the power to energize you and change your state of mind?

One of my energizers is a photo of one of my daughters holding a giant foam finger at a baseball game back when she was 11 years old. She has a silly look on her face and her hair is all over the place. It never fails to make me smile, no matter how bad my mood. Not only is it a precious memory of my daughter but looking at that picture makes me feel like I'm back at that game with her. It energizes me and propels me into the Approach State. It takes my mind off my current obstacles and energizes me long enough to right the ship.

That place for you might be a memory of a trip to the beach with your family or being out at the golf course with friends. The benefits of a prolonged existence in the Approach State include a higher EQ, increased influence, greater creativity, stronger interpersonal relationships, and better overall health.

How do you recognize your stressors to avoid acting irrationally? I remember some of the most common stressors with this acronym: HALT. It stands for:

H – Hungry

A – Angry

L – Lonely

T – Tired

I don't know about you, but at the end of a long workday, I am beat and know I just have to get home. It's not good. My wife used to tell me, "We can tell what kind of mood you're in the minute you walk in the door." Sometimes after a tough day, I'll pull into the park by my house, shut off the car, and just take some deep breaths. The point is to HALT, take inventory, and clear my mental filter before I walk through the door.

Remember that a leader possesses the highest level of emotional intelligence. To exist at that level, you must learn to maintain prolonged existence in the Approach State. It all goes back to understanding and mastering intrapersonal skills, and the first step in that process is the ability to recognize our influence on others. When you're in the Approach State, your influence increases, but it decreases when you're in the Avoid State. Whichever state of mind you reside in longer is the one that has the strongest influence on your relationships, job performance, energy level, and ultimately, your reputation.

Never forget the only thing separating the Approach State from the Avoid State is you. You have the ability to choose your state of mind. Sometimes, it doesn't feel like it and other times we don't want to hear it, but it always comes down to making that choice. When my daughters were in elementary school, I used to tell them their teachers won't make them mad, their friends won't make them sad, and ice cream won't make them glad. We all choose what we allow to influence us. We just have to take that first proactive step.

CHAPTER 3

PERSONAL AWARENESS

The central air conditioning unit in my house recently broke. Anyone who has been in that position knows how frustrating it can be, and it was something we had to get fixed.

My wife and I did our due diligence and all the necessary research before choosing a company with reasonable rates and good reviews. When the technician arrived, we headed outside. This guy walked up the driveway, but he didn't shake my hand or introduce himself—he didn't even look me in the eye. He walked straight up to the unit next to the house, gave everything a quick once over, pulled out his clipboard, and jotted some notes while uttering under his breath, "They expect me to get this done in one day? There's no way."

Okay. Nice to meet you too.

It was immediately clear to me that the technician struggled with personal awareness, an ability to recognize his influence on others. In other words, he didn't understand his influence on us and our situation. Let me back up because, in all fairness, I don't know anything about that technician. I don't know what was going through his mind or what kind of mood he was in. I don't know if he made an assumption based on the neighborhood I lived in or if he was having a bad day after dealing with a difficult customer. This happens to all of us, but regardless of the circumstances, his lack of personal awareness in that moment most likely stemmed from his feeling "less than."

What that technician didn't understand was that he was the only solution to a complex problem I was unable to solve on my own. I welcomed him with open arms because I was in a bind, and he was the only one who could help me in that moment. But as soon as he made me feel like an inconvenience, my confidence in his ability began to diminish.

Had he managed his frustrations and leveraged the skill of personal awareness, I would have trusted him to get to work and get the job done so my house could be cool again. But that's not how our exchange went down and immediately there was tension and friction between us.

The burden in this kind of situation doesn't always fall on the shoulders of the person who is providing the service. It's a two-way street, so the roles could easily have been reversed. Let's say the technician was outgoing, friendly, and eager to be helpful. What if he walked up the driveway with a smile and I was the one who snapped at him because I was in a hurry and needed the job done faster than realistically possible? In that case, I would have been the one not recognizing my influence and my image would deteriorate in his eyes.

The ability to recognize your influence on others goes far in determining the reputation of your company, yourself, and even your family. When a person lacks personal awareness, they lack integrity, which greatly diminishes their ability to lead.

Consider the Role You Play in Relationships

Understanding the influence you have on others may sound easy, but it's amazing how often we overlook our own behavior. Here's a RedRock Leadership training exercise I use with some of my clients. I ask them the following two questions and have them write answers in their workbook:

1. Think of someone with whom you have a good relationship. Describe his or her reputation and your energy level when you're around him or her.

2. Think of someone with whom you don't have a good relationship, though an improved relationship would benefit you. Describe that person's reputation and your energy level when you are around him or her.

After a couple of minutes, I'll go around the room and we'll discuss the answers to the first question—not the names of the people but their reputation and how they feel when they are around them. I'll hear adjectives like "energetic," "positive," "supportive," "kind," and "generous." It's easy to remain in the Approach State when you're around these people.

I do the same thing for the second question. The words used to describe that person are much different: "Dishonest," "pushy," "rude," "draining," "mean," and "unforgiving." When you're with this group of people, it's difficult to remain in the Approach State.

Next, I explain how the person in the second question is the answer to someone else's first question. It takes a while for that one to sink in but once it does it's an eye-opener. I ask the group, "Who's the common denominator?" They don't even have to answer. Their facial expressions say it all. *They* are the common denominator.

If you work in sales, when you make a cold call to a potential client you're likely entering the conversation as the person described in the second question. The same goes for those who have strained relationships with their colleagues and teammates.

If you've been playing along, think about the person you would pick as the answer to the second question. Do you think it's possible you could be causing that person to act the way they do toward you? Do you think if you change the way you approach that person your relationship could improve? I'm nowhere near perfecting it, but since coming up with this exercise, I've become more conscious about remaining in the Approach State while interacting with those I describe in the second question. Regardless of whether they rub me the wrong way or say something that infuriates me, I do my best to manage my emotions so I can keep from slipping into the Avoid State.

It's important for us to realize we have an influence on others, and when we slip into the Avoid State, that influence can quickly turn negative.

Leadership and Personal Awareness

Many outside factors can hinder our personal awareness and lead to us saying things that unintentionally hurt someone. This could have been what happened to Kevin's coach when he said Kevin would never be good enough to play basketball if he couldn't learn to do push-ups. If we stop to look around, we see it happening all the time.

Personally, I believe it's because we don't interact with each other as intimately as we have in the past. People often communicate over text, email, and instant messaging in a way that is less personal than speaking in person or on the phone. When it comes to social media, it's easy to project a false persona, so our insecurities surface when we have to engage with someone face-to-face. When this happens, we put up our guard and fall into the Avoid State.

There's no question that those emerging into leadership roles today are challenged when it comes to developing personal awareness. I notice this among the ninth graders of my Bible study group. Most of the young men in the group know each other really well, so if a new member isn't naturally outgoing, he often has a difficult time connecting.

That's what happened with Brent. During his first time with our group, he didn't say a word. He just sat in the corner and gave off the vibe that he didn't want to be there. I didn't want to single him out or put him on the spot because that would have made him feel even more uncomfortable. But when I saw him sitting by himself in the stairwell scrolling through his phone after class, I struck up a conversation with him.

"Hey, Brent, what's going on?"

Brent didn't even look up. He just grunted, "Eh."

"Eh? Come on, Brent. Put your phone down, and let's talk."

I didn't raise my voice because I didn't want to push him away. He put his phone down and began to open up. We actually had a very good talk, and I learned a lot about him in a short amount of time.

I would have handled that situation completely differently before I learned the skill of personal awareness. Because I thought he was behaving rudely, I probably would have been aggressive and said something like, "Brent, you need to listen to me. If you don't put that phone down, I'll take it away from you."

Some people would probably say I was coddling Brent, but I disagree. I was simply looking to create a positive relationship with him, and I knew I needed to recognize my influence on him personally. In doing so, I was also indirectly teaching him the skill of personal awareness.

Personal awareness is an important skill that we must all learn to improve. Your words and body language matter. Regardless of the situation, you want to sustain mental toughness and remain in the Approach State, especially in the company of negative individuals with whom you want to build stronger, more positive relationships. Being able to play nice in the sandbox requires a high level of personal awareness.

Remove Insecurity and the Sky Is the Limit

Personal awareness often stems from insecurity, and there's no better example of this than Adam, my longtime friend and former client.

I met Adam several years ago when he was in his twenties selling health insurance. The owner of his company called me and said, "Adam needs help. You need to train this guy. He just isn't making enough cold calls and he's not closing."

When I interviewed Adam, I could tell he wanted to get better, he just didn't know how. As we discussed his current situation and his challenges, he admitted that he had a lot to learn and decided to come work with me.

Adam decided to participate in one of my public training programs to improve his personal leadership and sales abilities. On his first day, he took a seat in the middle of the room and just stared at the whiteboard while I spoke. He was the only one in class who didn't take a single note. I really didn't think he was retaining anything I said. But the more time we spent together in coaching sessions, the more I realized that what I said was sinking in. It was a classic example of the trainer being trained.

I learned Adam is a highly visual person, so when I spoke, he'd run everything through his mind and project it on the board behind me. That's how he learns.

The more I got to know Adam, the more he opened up.

"Jeff, here's the problem. I'm making $60,000 a year. I want to be making $100,000," he confided in me. "My boss wants me to call on bigger companies, but bigger companies don't exist in the small town where I live."

He had already convinced himself he couldn't do it. He was in the Avoid State, convinced there was no way he would ever improve or make the money he wanted. I shared a Henry Ford quote with him: "Whether you think you can, or you think you can't, you're right."

I challenged him.

"Adam, is it that big companies don't exist, or is it that you don't see the big companies?" I asked.

"What do you mean?"

"Here's what I want you to do," I said. "The next time you go to a networking event, I want you to introduce yourself as someone who works specifically with companies who have more than 100 employees."

"Jeff, I'll never close another piece of business again!"

"Why do you say that?" I asked.

"Because I'm never at an event with companies that have more than 100 employees. I told you, those companies don't exist in my town."

"Adam, just give it a shot and see what happens."

A couple weeks later, he came back to see me.

"Jeff, I did what you said, and something interesting happened," Adam said. "When I was at this networking event, I had a couple people approach me after and say, 'My company only has 40 employees, but would you consider working with me?'"

"Do you see it now?"

"Yeah, a company with 40 employees is larger than the companies I've been working with."

"Don't stop there," I said. "The next time someone asks you if they are a large enough company for you, don't be so quick to say yes. Instead, ask if his or her company plans on being that large someday. This will encourage collaboration. That will require trust on your part, but as you trust and engage the individual, he or she will be more likely to do the same in return."

This was all a way for me to help him get rid of his insecurity and improve his personal awareness. A few weeks later, he came back to me and said it was all coming together.

"When I asked a woman who approached me if she wanted to have 100 or more employees someday, it actually seemed like she was more interested in working with me," he said.

Adam got stronger buy-in because he trusted the other person. The more often you trust, the more often you'll be trusted. That's how you build strong personal bonds.

Fast forward three years and Adam wasn't making $60,000 a year anymore, he was making more than $300,000, which put him in a position to impact even more people. That was well beyond what even he thought he was capable of.

It was incredibly rewarding to watch Adam's progress and see his influence, confidence, and leadership ability increase over the years. Eventually, he set out to accomplish his own goals and dreams by starting a sporting goods company to sell a product that he invented. Today, he is transforming the experiences of athletes everywhere.

How to Change Your Mindset

It can be a challenge to change your mindset, but here are three ways to get yourself into the Approach State:

Keep a journal. It sounds simple, but if you do it consistently, it can be an effective way to better understand and alter your mindset. Writing down your thoughts can reveal things about yourself, such as what you really think about what's going on around you. Sometimes journaling can help you figure out how your thoughts are holding you back. It's also a great way to reset your attitude at the beginning and end of each day.

One particular journaling exercise I like, I call "gratitude to shape my attitude." It's simply writing down 10 statements about what you're grateful for and then writing three action items from those 10 statements. I like to do this in the morning because it helps me get into the Approach State before I head into my day.

I had a client whose company was experiencing an extremely tumultuous time, and he really struggled to remain in the Approach State. I shared the idea of the gratitude journal, and he put his own twist on it. He found an accountability partner who did the same, and they would text their 10 statements to each other every morning. He cracked me up when he told me, "I can't believe you get paid for this, Ruby! This gratitude journal has transformed me. I've even had people telling me that something is different about me."

He went on to explain that he felt like he had more influence than ever before over difficult situations. He also said that he felt like he was expending less energy adapting to the chaos. He wasn't getting frustrated nor was he shutting down.

I hear these types of journaling success stories all the time. If you have a desire to spend more time in the Approach State, I strongly suggest you start journaling!

Use proactive language. The words you use matter. They shape your mindset and have an influence on your mood, confidence, and self-perception. It may not sound like a big deal but simply tweaking your vocabulary so you're using positive words instead of negative words can keep you in the Approach State.

Here are some simple changes that you can start making today to develop a more proactive vocabulary:

- **Hard:** "Hard" is defeatist. Instead, say something is "challenging" because we're all up for a challenge.

- **Try:** Remember in *Star Wars* when Yoda said, "Do or do not, there is no try." You either do something or you don't. Saying "try" is another way to prepare yourself for failure. That can cause you to become defensive and slip into the Avoid State.

- **Can't:** Any time you say "can't," it can almost always be replaced by "won't."

- **Maybe or Probably:** Both of these words are noncommittal. Decide to commit by saying either "yes" or "no."

- **But:** The word "but" negates everything you just said. Replace it with "and." Remain firm and state your point without feeling the need to appease or compromise.

Using definitive, proactive language keeps you in the Approach State and prevents you from inadvertently slipping into the Avoid State.

This can be challenging because often we don't even know we're being defeatist and negative, and it's natural for us to self-medicate with our language. What state of mind are you in when you say something like, "Easier said than done?" You're in the Avoid State. I used to catch myself saying this when I thought about putting my two daughters through college at the same time. It's the same thing with a phrase like, "I'll give this a try." Often when people use this phrase, they might as well not even try. They already set themselves up for failure. What's the point? Save your energy. If you eliminate the word "try," and say the word "will," it changes your entire perspective.

Self-medicating language can be instilled at a young age. I noticed this in my own kids several years ago when both of our girls were much younger. Whenever we'd jump in the car to go anywhere, my youngest would always say, "Can we stop for ice cream?"

My oldest daughter, who was 11 at the time and obviously wise beyond her years, would chime in and say, "We're not stopping for ice cream. We can't afford to stop for ice cream every time we get in the car."

My ears perked up when I heard that. Where does an 11-year-old learn to talk like that? It didn't take long to figure out that she probably got it from me so I made sure to chime in.

"Hold on honey, let me help you out here," I said. "It's not that we can't stop for ice cream, it's that we're choosing not to."

We often use these negative statements with our coworkers, clients, family members, colleagues, and friends to protect our insecure and weak mindsets. If we can focus instead on using proactive language, we'll find life more fulfilling.

Know your stressors and what triggers them. An Avoid State stressor can be like a flashback or a trigger that has the potential to cause an emotionally charged reaction. Stressors are personal, so they are different for everyone. What are yours? Write them down.

Here are some common stressors:

- Anniversary dates marking the loss of loved ones

- Police car lights

- Looming deadlines

- Feeling overwhelmed

- Family friction

- Being judged

- Getting criticized

- Being teased or put down

- Getting a big bill in the mail

- Overdrafting your checking account

- Not being listened to

- Being lied to

- Feeling hungry, angry, lonely, or tired (HALT)

The Power of the Approach State

Jake left his high-paying job as a software developer after one of his friends convinced him he'd be good at selling life insurance. Jake was making $150,000 a year, but he was swayed by a recruiter to take a job with a much lower base salary and a higher income ceiling. He thought it could be a way for him to better provide for his family, but he soon found that switching from a career as a software developer to a salesperson is like moving from quarterback to the defensive line—the two jobs couldn't be more different. Sure enough, he began to panic and doubt himself.

"Jeff, I don't know what to do," he told me. "They want me to make 100 cold calls every day. I can't do that."

There was that word—"can't." Right then, I identified his low personal awareness. In his mind, he was defeated before he got started. To help him get into the Approach State, I encouraged him to believe that when he picked up the phone, he was reaching out to a large group of people who needed what he had.

We started by changing his language. The job wasn't "hard," it was "challenging." He wasn't going to "try," he was going to "do." That was the first step in helping him overcome his insecurity about being a salesperson and speaking with strangers. I am certain that this is a fear he never had to confront before taking the sales job. Once he changed his language, his personal awareness increased and he was able to spend extended periods of time in the Approach State. This breakthrough allowed him to experience success.

With practice, we can learn to manage our emotions, though there will always be unavoidable situations when your thoughts and emotions overtake you. It's unreasonable to think that you'll be able to completely shelter yourself from these moments, but it's important to gain the knowledge necessary to maintain your composure at times when you are most volatile.

Emotional Hijacking

Everyone knows someone who is afraid of heights. When people with this fear walk across a bridge, look out the window of a highrise, or stand on a ladder, they get tense, their palms get sweaty, and they lose their composure. They may get irritable and even irrational, just thinking about one of these situations. Although they may be the epitome of calm, cool and collected in other situations, when they get more than 10 feet off the ground, they become a completely different person.

Why does this happen? In most cases, the fear of losing control overrides the ability to be rational. They are forced to relinquish control to whomever designed the bridge, building, or ladder, and they react and often panic.

This is how an emotional hijacking works. You enter a situation you perceive as stressful and your heart begins to race, your palms get sweaty, and your cognition is altered. You quickly turn from reasonable and rational to primal and reactive. The experience might leave your brain feeling cloudy for hours.

An emotional hijacking is often referred to as an "amygdala hijacking," a term first coined by *Emotional Intelligence* author Daniel Goleman,[1] since that is essentially what happens in the brain during crisis. The amygdala is the part of the brain that helps regulate our

1 http://www.gostrengths.com/what-is-an-amygdala-hijack/

"flight or fight" reaction when our brain senses imminent danger and releases stress hormones.

During an emotional hijacking, our body prevents us from making rational decisions.[2] Someone in the midst of an emotional hijacking may become reactive and extremely defensive as he or she lashes out at stressors. If the stressor is another person, things can get ugly real quick.

Emotional hijacking is a term everyone needs to understand, especially those who hold leadership positions. It's imperative that these individuals learn how to avoid being emotionally hijacked in order to experience long-term success. The level at which you're able to accomplish this is directly correlated with your EQ, which increases as you improve personal awareness, integrity, internal motivation, empathy, and social skills.

In my experience, the difference between a company that is thriving and a company that is just surviving is the level of its leadership team's emotional intelligence. When faced with a challenging situation that isn't going to have a win-win outcome, leaders learn to walk away before reacting irrationally.

Being emotionally hijacked is avoidable and increasing your EQ is possible. Committing to both will not only help you become a stronger person but a true leader. To improve your EQ, you want to look at other aspects of your life, including sleep, exercise, and your personal habits. The more organized you are personally, the easier it will be to identify and deal with your stressors, manage your emotions, and remain in the Approach State.

---

2 https://blog.ttisuccessinsights.com/emotional-intelligence-prevents-amgydala-hijack

How to Get into the Approach State

It's easy for me to tell you to be more aware and to live life in the Approach State but if it were really that easy, everybody would do it and my job wouldn't exist. Remember, my business exists because these are problems that plague business owners, managers, employees, and even entire companies.

Wouldn't it be great if we could be doing what we enjoy all the time without conflict so we were happy and content and never left the Approach State? Sure, it would, but life doesn't work that way.

Unfortunately, there's no switch to flip to return your mind to the Approach State after an emotional hijacking. When this happens, it's too late, but there's a technique I use when I'm confronted by one of my stressors to help keep me in a rational state of mind. It's called STAR.

S – Stop

T – Think

A – Assess

R – Respond

We all have difficult people in our lives who bring out the worst in us. This makes me think of one particular person, one of my former clients. This guy was my kryptonite; his ultra-critical ways just seemed to rub me the wrong way. One of my stressors was seeing his name pop up on my phone. I dreaded those phone calls.

One day, I had a breakthrough. Instead of avoiding his call, I decided to STAR. When I answered his call from the Approach State,

I was able to respond rationally and logically. I made it a point to really take a genuine interest in him, in a way I hadn't before. I asked him about his day and what was going on. Not only did we have a productive conversation, for the first time since I could remember, I wasn't in the Avoid State when I got off the call. I admit I was a bit worn out because it took some energy for me to adapt but it was a good kind of worn out. During our conversation, I actually developed a newfound respect for him.

Don't mistake STAR for being an instant fix. There are many times you will STAR and not have a positive outcome. The question is, can you hold it together? If you STAR and it doesn't work at first, don't punish yourself. Only punish yourself for inaction, never punish yourself for failure. It's absolutely possible to do all the right things and still not succeed. What's most important is that you take action. Be real with yourself. Did you persevere and do everything you thought possible at the time? If so, you have nothing to regret. There's always a chance the work you put in might pay off in an unforeseen way down the road.

CHAPTER 4

INTEGRITY

When I ask a room full of people, during RedRock Leadership training, if they believe they operate with a high level of integrity, which is when our intentions match our actions, everyone thinks they do. We often associate integrity with honesty and trustworthiness, which is part of integrity. But it's difficult, if not impossible, for anyone to be honest and trustworthy all the time.

Enter a stressor and it's a whole new ball game. This is when our personal awareness drops and we naturally try to cover up our insecurities, which results in a breach in our integrity.

It happens to all of us, and to illustrate this point, I'll ask clients to think of a time when their intentions didn't match their actions. If they're still having trouble and I have to prod them, I'll have them think of scenarios when they knew they needed to apologize. That opens their minds and gets them thinking. Maybe they hurt someone's feelings without realizing it, which is an example of when intentions don't match actions. Then I'll ask what happened, and it almost always either led to an argument or broke trust. Trust is the big one. Whenever your intentions don't match your actions, you've given the other person a reason not to trust you.

When someone close to you points out when your intentions don't match your actions, it really hammers the point home. For me, that was my wife. I have a great marriage today, but when my wife and I were younger, we were still finding our way and learning each other's idiosyncrasies. If you're married, you know exactly what I'm talking about.

I've been a salesman for most of my life, so for me, two plus two doesn't always equal four. I grew up believing I could bend the truth one way or another to get things to go my way. Back when I was 19, I sold 45 vacuum cleaners in three months walking door-to-door. I'm not proud of this but I was able to sell those vacuum cleaners not because I believed in what I was selling but because I learned the pitch. When I executed the pitch, it was like I couldn't fail. I had no clue if I was selling a good vacuum or a bad one but I got people to believe me. That mentality was hardwired into my brain.

My wife is not a salesperson. She's analytical and very literal, so for her, two plus two always equals four. It shouldn't be a surprise that my way of thinking didn't always match up with hers. It took me some time to realize it, but those differences became the source of a lot of friction. Whenever I did something that upset her, I would apologize and tell her that I would never do it again.

Guess what? It would happen again. We'd get into an argument. I'd apologize and say that I'd never do it again. Things would be good for a while, and guess what? You got it. The same thing would happen again. Finally, after about three or four times, my wife called me out. "If you're really sorry, you would change your actions."

She was right. I wasn't being honest with her, or myself. It reminds me of when I was a kid and my mom used to tell me, "Don't lie because eventually you will start to believe your own lies." Lies can evolve into a character flaw without you even realizing it. Think about it, nobody steals just once. Chances are if someone steals from you, he or she will steal again. The same is true about bad habits and lies that may seem innocuous at first but grow over time, reflecting poorly on your character and ultimately your reputation.

Picture an iceberg. The 15 percent that sticks out of the water is your reputation. What people don't see is the 85 percent below the surface—that's your character. My wife's comment about changing my actions stuck with me because I'd been lying to myself. Deep down, I wanted to change and be better for her. To do this, I needed to make a conscious decision to work on my character and align my actions with my words.

Managing Stressors

What habits or patterns would you like to change about yourself? It could be anything. Maybe you want to stop being passive. Maybe you have the opposite problem and don't want to be overly aggressive. You might want to stop holding people to unrealistically high expectations.

For me, a big problem was bending the truth. I was notorious for being late. At first, I started making excuses for why I was late, but after a while, I found myself flat out lying about why I was late. That's not good. It adds up. It was an obvious breach of integrity that I needed to eliminate. You have to be honest with yourself and properly identify things you need to change. If you expect to lead others, you can't lack integrity because people won't trust you. As you know by now, it always comes back to trust.

It's much more difficult to recognize breaches of integrity that seem to be out of your control. Just like with an emotional hijacking, the key to maintaining integrity in the most difficult situations is to recognize the stressors that can set you off. Sometimes all you have to do is listen to your body to know when you're approaching the Avoid State where you're likely to experience a breach of integrity.

You'll know you're moving into the Avoid State when you...

- Find yourself in a situation that makes you nervous.

- Feel yourself beginning to grimace or tighten your eyes.

- Begin to have feelings that typically lead to an issue.

- Hear words that indicate you've stepped into a problem.

- Are having thoughts that are negative.

There will also be signs that only you will recognize. I know I'm heading for trouble when I find myself moving to the front of my chair and leaning forward. For you, it might be when you lean back and slouch. Pay attention and be conscious of your emotions and how they're expressed through your body's nonverbal cues.

It's also important to be aware of nonverbal stressors. Being able to read another person's body language can help you get out in front of any conversation so you don't become nervous and suffer a breach of integrity. It's easy to misinterpret, however. That's why it's important that you STAR to keep yourself from slipping into the Avoid State where you could make negative assumptions and say something you regret.

The phrase I rely on in these situations is, "If you feel it, STAR and say it." Some people think this might get them into trouble, but for me, I'd much rather diffuse a potentially explosive situation sooner rather than later. If I see someone zoning out during a conversation, I might think I said something to upset him or her so I'll stop to ask if anything is wrong. Most of the time, the other person will admit he or she was just distracted and thinking about something else. Had I not asked and just plowed through the warning signs, I could have built up animosity in my mind and suffered a breach of integrity. Calling out the moment allows me to reset and get the other person's undivided attention.

This works on a much larger scale too. Have you ever worked with someone who did something to get under your skin? If you let it go day after day, that negative energy and frustration builds up until one day you snap, or worse, say or do something you'll regret later. Those are breaches of integrity that can be avoided if you address issues up front and early.

Remember, these skills are interconnected. The best way to improve your integrity is to improve your personal awareness.

Build Your Culture with Integrity

Craig began to turn things around at J-TEK International once his intentions began matching his actions. I helped him develop a strategic business plan to help him remain in the Approach State. The strategic business plan included a clear vision for the future. Next, he created goals to support that vision and a strategy to support his goals. Finally, he created detailed action steps and tracking measures for accountability to support the action steps.

At first, Craig didn't trust his team at all. To get him started, I told him, "Craig, you don't have to trust your team just yet. Let's start by trusting the process."

As Craig modified his behavior, he spent more time in the Approach State and he learned to trust the process. This eventually led him to a point where he started trusting his team. Craig and Monica attended RedRock Leadership training together and developed a common language. Shortly after, they enrolled their entire sales team in RedRock Leadership training.

Monica eventually began to oversee the sales team without Craig's day-to-day involvement. Craig eventually changed Monica's title from "Sales Manager" to "Sales Team Leader." He stopped referring to his people as employees and began referring to them as "members of his team." He even went so far as to collaborate with Monica to create a sales budget. Then they got rid of individual sales quotas so that everyone on the sales team could create a sales business plan. In those plans, each sales team member set his or her own expectations for sales revenue and profit that aligned with the company's overall sales budget. The team began to look forward to their bimonthly sales meetings, which are now led by Monica, and they all work to accomplish the goals they established together.

Once Craig pointed Monica and the sales team in the right direction, they worked to bring the RedRock Leadership principles, concepts, and common language to the rest of the company. Today, everyone in the company holds each other accountable to their goals and objectives.

After several months of J-TEK moving in a very positive direction, they were tested when Monica hired Michael. Monica thought Michael had great potential. He was a "give me the ball and let me run with it" kind of guy, but Michael didn't take to the RedRock Leadership training nor did he adhere to his team's common language. He also didn't take the time to understand how the company went to market. He would short-circuit the sales process and move right to discounting just to get an order.

His behavior went against the grain of the culture at J-TEK International, and it didn't go unnoticed. Other members of the sales team began to call Michael out for offering to cut pricing to get business.

"What you're doing is a breach of integrity," a sales team member finally told Michael. "That's not how we solve our clients' problems here. All you're doing is trying to get a sale for yourself. We'd rather lose a deal and save a relationship instead of doing a deal that might hurt the company, just to get a paycheck."

It worked because shortly after that, Michael resigned. After this experience, Craig told me how impressed he was with Monica and the sales team. He saw all of their hours invested in RedRock Leadership training paying off. The culture had become so strong that it literally spit Michael out.

"You're becoming a true leader, Craig!" I said.

More importantly, he was beginning to realize he didn't always have to step in and be the hero. The company was starting to grow, and Craig was finally building a legacy.

How Integrity Can Help Your Business

To build a loyal following, it's in your best interest to have a personal connection between what you do for a living and your audience or customer base.

In his book *Start with Why*, motivational speaker Simon Sinek explains the importance of communicating "why" before communicating "how" and "what." No matter what your company does, if you're going to get people to buy in and identify with what you provide, your sales team must learn to communicate from the inside out. This will prove that your intentions match your actions, and it's how your customers and potential customers will ultimately learn to trust you.

Due to the furious pace of change, companies today have less time to gain customer trust in their products and services, and they must constantly change to keep their attention. Look at the way Apple does it. Steve Jobs used to say that he wanted to challenge the status quo with everything his company did. He did, and it worked! Think about how many people religiously trust Apple whenever they come out with new products.

Without integrity you won't build trust.

You Have to Make Tough Decisions

Don't expect all of this this to be easy, and be prepared to deal with a fair amount of drama.

Take my client Ted, for example. Ted owned a private equity firm and mentored a young guy named Justin, who was brought into his company to work the phones and scout potential clients. Ted enrolled Justin in RedRock Leadership training, and he moved up fast in the company. Within a year, Justin was doing very well for himself. Maybe too well, as pride got the best of him.

Justin found himself in a deep conversation with one of the firm's largest clients, Janet, the CEO of a large tool-and-die company. Justin's dad owned a manufacturing company, so he had experience in that world. He spun a good story, and Janet bought it and wound up offering Justin a job as her General Manager.

When Justin told Ted about the opportunity with Janet, an alarm went off. When Ted discovered Janet had flown Justin out to Atlanta to have dinner with her and her team, he was clearly shaken up. He felt betrayed. Ted invested a lot of time and energy into mentoring Justin. He even thought Justin might take over for him one day.

Ted called me and said that he wanted to talk to Janet and put a stop to this, but I helped Ted understand that even though he felt betrayed, clearly Justin wasn't content at his company. Although Justin was doing a great job and making Ted a profit, he operated as a loner. In addition, having this type of secret dialogue with a client was inappropriate and certainly a violation of the company's core values.

I asked Ted if that was the foundation on which he wanted to build his company. He admitted to me that being taken advantage of was one of his stressors. Once he got back into the Approach State, he was able to realize that his relationship with Justin wasn't going to be a win-win, so Ted decided to wash his hands of the situation. He told Justin to take the job.

Three weeks later, Ted got a call from Janet. After apologizing for taking Justin away from his company, she let Ted know that things didn't work out. Justin clearly didn't know as much as he said he did and wound up making some pretty big mistakes in a very short period of time, which put her company under significant strain. She had no choice but to let him go.

Justin realized that he had messed up. He called Ted and said, "I'm sorry. I had a breach of integrity, and my intentions didn't match my actions." I'm not kidding. That's what he said, word-for-word. In his own effort to maintain integrity, Ted didn't offer Justin his job back, and you know what? His business never skipped a beat.

Justin made a mistake, just like we all have. I've had several breaches of integrity in my life. It's part of the human condition, but one of the best things we can do when we mess up is to learn from our mistakes and make corrections so it's less likely to happen in the future. As for Ted, it wasn't an easy decision for him to refuse to rehire his star performer, but it was the right move for both of them.

CHAPTER 5

INTERNAL MOTIVATION

E very skill of emotional intelligence is connected to another.

A high level of personal awareness allows us to recognize the impact we have on others in any given situation. The more aware we are, the less likely we are to have a breach of integrity. In order to maintain that integrity during difficult-to-manage situations, we must have strong internal motivation. This is also known as intrinsic motivation, or a deep drive or desire to do the right things for the right reasons. This is the opposite of extrinsic motivation, which is nothing more than a desire to avoid punishment or a yearning to gain a reward such as recognition, success, influence, or money.

Internal motivation is a critical aspect of mental toughness and a high EQ. It's what keeps you going when external issues and problems arise so you can move past them. It makes it easier to stay the course when you're passionate about and believe in what you're doing.

To better understand the intricacies of internal motivation, let's consider a 1975 study conducted by psychologists Edward Deci and

Richard Ryan at the University of Rochester,[3] which found that people have three innate psychological needs. Everyone needs to feel:

- Competent

- Heard

- Autonomous

Internal motivation intensifies as these needs are fulfilled. Deci and Ryan explain that when people feel competent, heard, and autonomous, they freely seek what interests them. It's under these conditions that a person makes the conscious decision to engage and commit to helping your organization succeed. When internal motivation is well-developed, people learn to persevere and trust their ability to conquer day-to-day challenges.

Here's a real-life example to take into consideration. Angie, a saleswoman, was doing very well, hitting her numbers month after month. Then all of the sudden, she went into a sales slump. At the same time, her husband lost his job, and they found themselves in a tough financial situation. Even though she received a salary, her commissions had dropped and the couple could barely cover their monthly household bills. Soon she became obsessed with the idea that she would lose her job, too.

Instead of prospecting for new business, she spent time following up on old customer estimates and proposals. In an effort to be more visible to management, she also arrived early and stayed late at work because she was desperately afraid of getting fired and losing her salary.

---

3 https://msu.edu/~dwong/StudentWorkArchive/CEP900F01-RIP/Webber-IntrinsicMotivation.htm

Well, guess what happened? After several months of not hitting her numbers, she was eventually let go for lack of performance. Angie's lack of internal motivation actually cost her job. In the end, she wasn't doing the right things for the right reasons.

Establish Your Core Values

Core values are fundamental principles and beliefs that guide your actions and behavior. They define your priorities and keep you on the right track so you can improve the skills necessary to increase your EQ and maintain a prolonged existence in the Approach State.

In years past, the concept of creating core values was a marketing stunt. It was an attempt to show the outside world you have a strong ethical and moral foundation. They were posted on websites, but nobody in the company actually knew they existed. That's changed. It's no longer marketing's responsibility, but the responsibility of those in a position of leadership to clearly establish and advocate core company values. This is why creating core values is a foundational aspect of RedRock Leadership training. If people who work with you know and believe in what you stand for, there's a stronger likelihood that they'll be internally motivated, which will nurture success.

"Is there any way to fix my people?" That's a question I hear from many business owners. And their stories are all very similar. Some of these companies have been in business for many years yet continue to struggle with profitability and employee turnover. As with J-TEK International, the owner blames the members of his or her team instead of looking inward and taking responsibility.

Getting those in a position of leadership to recognize that they're the problem can be a challenge. One of the key components of solidifying a culture is helping people develop and adhere to the core values of the organization, even if they start out resistant to the idea.

It's leadership's responsibility to support and promote the company's core values, while pointing everyone in the organization to a positive future. If they don't, individuals will pull back—especially during rocky times—and focus only on what's important to themselves personally. In turn, the company culture will deteriorate, and teams will disintegrate. Determination, respect, responsibility, effort, preparedness, and diligence are all examples of core values. How can you determine yours?

Step 1: List up to 10 negative traits that can lead to poor performance. They may include some or all of your stressors.

Laziness, negativity, and tardiness are all items that pop up on most everyone's list. Be sure to list ones that may be unique to you and your world.

Step 2: State the opposite of these 10 traits.

If you wrote lazy, negative, and tardy, you would now write the opposite, such as energetic, positive, and punctual. A quick note: If any version of the words honesty or trust appears on your list, either look for different words or cross them out. Honesty and trustworthiness are broad terms and should be at the root of all your core values, so focus your attention on identifying other more specific values.

Step 3: Group the opposite-traits into three groups by considering what they have in common.

It's not unusual for some people to overthink this step. If you're a highly structured person, you may struggle categorizing these actions into three groups. But if you're a free thinker, it will flow a little easier. You can be objective or subjective. Either way, focus less on being perfect and more on making them personal.

Step 4: Name each group (each group is one of your core values).

Some people want to have four or five groups, but I've found that it's difficult to remember more than three. These three words should describe the fundamental principles and beliefs that you want to guide your organization's actions and behaviors.

Step 5: Define each core value.

Provide the meaning of each of your three core values. Once you've memorized and internalized them, share the core values with your team and make them visible for all to see. Remember, this is not for marketing purposes. This is to keep you and your team accountable for improving internal motivation. Many people create a mission statement using their core values to tie it all together, which is an excellent idea.

Our core values at RedRock Leadership are:

- **Prepared.** We realize this is how we will achieve the greatest efficiency for ourselves and our clients.

- **Determined.** We are committed to accomplishing our goals on time, regardless of any challenges.

- **Diligent.** We visualize all tasks as special assignments and focus our energy on accomplishing them.

With our core values in mind, we decided on this as our mission statement: "To be faithful to God while serving others and being excellent in all we do."

Your Core Values Will Ground You

If you're a determined person, you know what a challenge it can be to remain in the Approach State for long periods of time. It's great to be motivated and driven, but when times get tough, it's easy to become disoriented and lose perspective.

For the first 35 years of my life, I was determined to be the best and have the most, like many people. However, the more successful we are, the more responsibility falls on our shoulders as the tower we're building gets higher and higher. All the while, we become more protective of that tower and find ourselves acting more and more like laggards or, at best, loners. Without even realizing it, we become motivated by external factors like money, success, power, and influence. We get a taste of those things and want more. It's human nature. This often goes hand-in-hand with developing a defensive mindset. What we don't realize at the time is that when we are extrinsically motivated, we're building a house of cards.

When it comes to internal motivation, I believe there are two types of people: those who are focused on taking as much as they can out of this life and those who are focused on putting as much into life as they can. Leaders have a well-developed skill of internal motivation and are focused on the latter. Getting here can be a challenge, especially given the culture of the world we live in today. It's not unusual for someone to experience transformation before they really develop this skill. That's what it took for me.

I experienced transformation when I was 35 years old. I was sitting with a friend in a coffee shop having one of those "meaning of life" conversations. He was a Christian, and I wasn't, not yet anyway. I was earning and accomplishing more than ever before, yet my level of joy and happiness were not growing in proportion to my level of success.

Through our conversation, he helped me understand that I was created for a purpose on purpose and that God, my Creator, actually had a plan for me. As we talked, I realized that God's plan for my life was likely much different than the plan I had for myself.

My friend went on to show me how the Bible points out that I am born separated from God, a sinner destined for a life of consumption that would ultimately lead to exiting this life within the next 70 or 80 years. Then he went on to show me how Jesus, God himself, came into this world to live a perfect life and die in my place so that I could live with him eternally.

No wonder I was so focused on taking all I could out of the world. The plan I had for myself had me, hopefully, living for 70 or 80 years. God's plan had me living for eternity. That blew my mind. Eternity?

As I learned more, I believed it and my faith began taking root. This is how my transformation took place. I am here to tell you that I have never been the same since. Today, because of my faith, whenever I become disoriented and find myself overly concerned with my status, bank account, and reputation, I focus on my internal motivation and its connection to my belief system. This is when I shift from extrinsic to intrinsic.

Remember my mission? It's to be faithful to God while serving others and being excellent in all I do. I find that when I have an eternal perspective, I'm able to remain in the Approach State. It hasn't always been that way for me. It took me a very long time to understand that I'm much better off when I'm intentional and focused and when every critical decision I make in life is made with an eternal perspective in respect to my relationship with Christ.

If we're not principle-centered, we'll end up taking the burning issue of a particular moment and make it the center of our life. For example, if you can't afford to pay a bill, finances will become your focus. This is likely to cause other areas of your life to suffer until you get back on track financially. It's important to keep your priorities in order. What's more important is to identify the well from which they are all fed. That keeps everything in balance.

Being principle-centered helps you decide which job you're going to take, which job candidate you're going to hire, where you will spend your time, how you will invest your money, etc. All of these decisions are made based on what is most important to you. Everything comes back and connects to that center hub. If you live these life priorities and are more intentional about each one, life slows down, and it's more difficult to lose focus.

If you're in a job or in a relationship that does not align with your core values, then your priorities are going to suffer. And when your priorities suffer, ultimately, you won't accomplish the goals you set out to achieve. But if those core values actively influence you and you commit to living by them, they will become part of the internal motivation you need to live a life of integrity.

Core Values Will Define Your Culture

Shortly after starting RedRock Leadership, I created a recruiting division. There were so many business owners telling me they needed to hire better people that it seemed like a natural add-on. We recruited people who appeared to be better than those they had, but they didn't work out. It proved to be a trap that could have sunk the business. What was going on? Where was I going wrong?

That's when a light bulb went off in my head. Wait a minute! The people weren't the problem in my clients' companies. The problem was their culture. So, I put my foot down and refused to do any more recruiting until I knew they had taken the time to define their culture with clearly stated core values. Today, we do provide recruiting services in conjunction with the creation of a custom job benchmark, which defines the culture of the job, company, and candidate before the search begins. This has proven to be an extremely effective way to help organizations solidify and stabilize their culture. If you would like to know more about the RedRock Custom Job Benchmarking Process, go to RedRockLeadership.com/custom-job-benchmark.

When I help leadership teams create business plans, they create core values that define their culture. Many times the idea of promoting core values is met with resistance because some think that the approach is too soft, while others claim it's too restrictive. Instead of creating and promoting core values, many people want to create and implement more rules, systems, and processes because they think that's what will keep people in line. And there are others who simply don't want to rock the boat. These are typical responses, and it's also deflection, because these business owners know once they announce their core values, all eyes will be on them to live up to them.

Then something interesting happens. After the core values are announced and the culture starts to take shape, the business owner will pull me aside and say, "I'm beginning to wonder if I'm the reason we haven't been growing." They begin to question whether or not they really had the "people problem" they once thought, and they finally begin to understand it wasn't their people who were broken, it was their culture. The painful part is seeing them blame themselves for the problem.

They ask, "Can we fix it?"

I reply, "Absolutely!"

I tell them the first step in repairing a dysfunctional culture is to create and define your core values. However, I also make sure to let them know a big part of repairing the culture is getting people to succeed on their own accord. Of course, they're hesitant at first, but once we begin making progress, they buy in quickly.

This is what happened at J-TEK. Craig was all in. He decided to make it as easy as possible for everyone involved, so he met with each team and gave everyone a folder. On the left side of the folder was a document listing the company's core values and their definitions. Craig included a list of his goals and vision for the company, a short mission statement, and a summary of the company's strategy moving forward. On the right side of the folder was a severance package. He wanted to give them a choice.

Craig stood up in front of the entire company and told everyone, "I want you all to stay, but I realize there has been a lot of change over the past couple years. Even though I want you to trust me, I understand some of you might not be able to do that, which is why you have a choice."

He explained how the document on the left was an invitation to stay. Those who were committed to staying on board were asked to sign off on the core values. If they weren't on board or didn't think they were a good fit for the culture, he would essentially pay them to leave the company with a severance package based on their years of service. That's one way to send a clear message about expectations and ensure everyone is on the same page.

Only two people opted out. One was a young woman who had at one point asked Craig to move her from shipping and receiving to sales because she wanted to try something new, but she was in over her head. She realized that she wasn't a good fit for the culture, so she accepted the severance. It was best for all involved.

Another was a salesman who was on an island of his own, a loner. He was a college friend of Craig's who never seemed to fit in at J-TEK. As he read through the documents in the folder, it became clear he wasn't a good fit for the company's newly defined culture, so he accepted the severance package as well.

One of the more interesting aspects about working with J-TEK was how well Charles responded. As you may remember, Charles was the senior sales rep who felt frustrated because he thought Craig was destroying what his father and grandfather had built. He loved the idea of the stated core values. Charles also liked the idea of a more collaborative workplace, and within about six months of signing off on the core values, his sales increased by 25 percent. He proved to be a great fit for the culture and the overall work environment.

Using Core Values as a Guide

I got a call from Craig shortly after he committed to revamping his entire company culture. It turned out that Monica, who oversees the sales team, sent out an email unveiling her new cell phone policy. According to the email, there would be disciplinary action for anyone caught using his or her cell phone during work hours.

"I see she's working to increase productivity, but you taught me some things that make me think she shouldn't have done it the way she did," Craig said.

"Have her retract the email," I said. "I'm on my way now. Let's meet with Monica, then we'll call an impromptu team meeting, and I'll take it from there."

"What are you going to say?"

"Don't worry. We'll fix it."

When I got there, I huddled up with Craig and Monica.

"No matter what, please don't interrupt me, everything is going to work out fine." I said. "If it looks like I'm going up in flames, just believe me, I'm not."

Once the entire team was together, I told them, "I know that Monica retracted her email, and now we want to have a conversation with you about the cell phone policy."

I projected J-TEK's core values from my computer to the large monitor in the front of the room.

"Everyone here plays an important part in helping to protect the quality of this work environment," I said. "The way we do that is by upholding these core values."

So far, everyone was following me.

I continued, saying, "As far as the cell phone policy goes, if you believe that using your phone to access social media and text family and friends from work is going to help you be more productive at work, then use your phone as much as you need to." I continued to point out all of the things they could be doing and never once mentioned what they shouldn't be doing.

A couple of individuals seemed to have difficulty understanding what I was saying. One member of the team finally spoke up.

"I get it. I think I know what you're saying," the team member said. "You want us to make our own decision to put down our cell phones."

"Correct," I replied. "By looking at these core values, you can figure out the right thing to do."

During RedRock Leadership training sessions, I tell a story about one of the young men I mentor. He had been watching me for a number of years and knows that I don't drink alcohol, and haven't since 2007, for a number of reasons. When he turned 21, he asked me if I thought it was okay for him to have a drink.

I told him, "Well, you are legally allowed to drink, so if you believe that drinking is going to make you someone whom you need to be and you're convinced that it's going to help you be more productive in life, then you should drink."

"Mr. Jeff?"

"It's your decision, but you need to let your core values guide your actions and behavior," I said. "Don't do things because other people want you to do them and don't do them because other people tell you not to do them, either. You should do them because they align with your core values." That conversation led him to write down and define his core values and personal mission statement to help guide his behavior and actions.

It's the same thing with the cell phone policy. If we could get members of the J-TEK sales team to make their own decisions about adhering to the company's core values, then we could get them to take ownership—and also improve their internal motivation. It used to be that policies, rules, and regulations governed the workplace. It doesn't need to be like that anymore. If you take the time to establish guidelines and trust your people to uphold the core values of the organization while you work with them to strengthen the culture, you'll collectively achieve a higher level of internal motivation. This is when you'll really notice your culture transform.

As people's internal motivation grows stronger, they find themselves focused on doing the right things for the right reasons. It's an amazing feeling when you see your team make a decision to act upon the world instead of letting the world act upon them.

CHAPTER 6

EMPATHY

W hen someone tells me they don't have any empathy, I'll say, "Yes, you do. It's just smothered by how much you think about yourself." A lack of empathy is self-centeredness and an inability to recognize and respond to others' emotions. That's all it is. If you can eliminate self-centeredness, you can improve your ability to be empathetic.

In fact, research shows that the capacity to feel what another person feels is "hard-wired" through what are called "mirror neurons."[4] A functional magnetic resonance imagery (fMRI) measures brain activity and lights up regions of the brain when there's awareness of another person's pain or distress or when emotions and physical sensations are observed. This proves that each of us can absolutely share another person's emotions.[5]

During RedRock Leadership training sessions, we discuss three types of empathy:

- Emotional Empathy
- Cognitive Empathy
- Compassionate Empathy

---

4 http://www.livescience.com/health/050427_mind_readers.html
5 https://www.psychologytoday.com/us/blog/the-new-resilience/201004/are-you-suffering-empathy-deficit-disorder

Emotional empathy is an unconscious drive to respond to another person's emotions. You've probably witnessed how emotional empathy works with children. It's contagious. When one baby starts crying, babies nearby often start crying, too.

It works with adults as well. Think of how one person can influence someone else's mood. If you're in a bad mood, one interaction with a happy, smiling person can make you laugh and brighten your day. It works the other way, too. When our dog, Buckeye, passed away, everyone in our family responded to each other with emotional empathy. When one of us started crying, we all cried. It was as if we couldn't turn off the tears. It was because we "caught" each other's emotions and unconsciously responded in an instinctive and primitive way.

Cognitive empathy is a conscious ability to accurately assess and respond to someone else's emotional state. It's a type of empathy that takes effort to develop because it doesn't always come naturally.

Establishing your core values is crucial to ensure every member of your team is on board and working toward the same goal. But before you dismiss people who don't fit your culture, take the time to figure out if there is an issue that can be resolved. Everyone has stuff going on in their lives, and if you take the time to understand and empathize, you can help individuals better acclimate to the culture and ultimately be more productive.

Brenda was an inside salesperson at one of the companies with which I worked. One day, John, the owner of the company, called me about what he considered a serious situation.

"It seems like Brenda heads to the bathroom at 4:30 every day and changes into her workout clothes," he said. "Then she goes back to her desk, sits there for another half hour, and leaves right at 5 o'clock."

"Okay." I had to keep myself from chuckling. What was this all about?

"I'm getting sick and tired of it," he said. "It doesn't seem like she wants to be here."

"Really? Did you talk to her about it and ask why she's putting on her workout clothes before 5 o'clock?"

"No, I'm afraid if I approach her about it things will turn ugly. Can you help me?" he asked.

So, I met with Brenda. I learned she worked as a high school volleyball coach for four months out of the year. Practice was at 5:30 in Tampa, and her office was in St. Petersburg, so it was tough for her to arrive on time for practice at that hour.

"Usually I'm a little late, but I have a parent cover for me," she said.

I went back to John. I told him about the situation and proposed a solution.

"How about I tell her that she can leave at 4:30?" I asked.

"What? No! That's the whole problem."

"This will work."

"What will the rest of the team think?"

"I bet they'll think it's a really good thing."

It took a little bit more convincing, but I got John to agree to the plan and presented Brenda with the proposal.

"Brenda, it's great that you're coaching, but it's not safe for you to try and make it all the way to Tampa in 30 minutes during rush hour," I said. "We want to make sure that you can get there safely and on time, so how about you leave work at 4:30?"

"Oh, my goodness! Really?"

"Absolutely," I said.

"I can come in early and make up my time if you need me to," Brenda said.

"Just make sure you hit your sales numbers. That's what we need from you."

She was already hitting her sales numbers, and I was confident she would continue to do so. I then spoke to the rest of the team to make sure everything was out in the open. They all knew what was going on, and they were completely good with it. Had we done all of this on the down-low, it would have been a different story and could have easily created animosity or resentment. When people start to think that others are receiving special advantages or benefits, especially if they're kept a secret, they become discouraged and enter the Avoid State.

Over the course of the next three months, Brenda's sales went up. She became the model representative of the company culture. She was there early and on days she didn't have practice, she stayed late. She even talked up the company to her peers. Everything changed, and it was because we demonstrated cognitive empathy. If John had fired Brenda because he thought she was cutting corners without learning why, he would have lost a great team member and his business would have suffered. He would have been hard-pressed to find somebody to replicate the value she adds today.

John was blown away. First, he couldn't figure out why no one else was jealous. But when you're transparent, lead with encouragement, and do the right thing by taking care of people, it always works to your advantage. Cognitive empathy builds trust. But be careful. I'm not suggesting you suddenly go out and give in to everyone's demands. Instead, take proactive action to help people figure out how they can best manage their lives.

Cognitive empathy is considered a foundational skill of leadership. To be a leader you must be interested and aware of what's going on in the lives of others. As you recognize and understand the emotions of others with good intentions, you'll gain the insights you need.

Have you ever heard of the concept of an emotional bank account? Think about how a regular bank account works. Deposits are made, and this is how we save up money. When there's money in your bank account, you feel secure and have a certain sense of freedom. An emotional bank account works the same way, but it uses positive feelings instead of money. When the balance in your emotional bank account is high, communication with others is almost effortless because trust exists. Conversely, when the balance in your emotional bank account is low, trust deteriorates and communication suffers.

As a leader, you can leverage the skill of cognitive empathy by using words of affirmation to inspire and encourage those around you. When you do this, you make deposits into their emotional bank accounts. Try it! I believe you'll find that emotional deposits have a much greater return on investment than financial deposits ever could.

Compassionate empathy takes cognitive empathy one step further by recognizing another's emotions and sincerely acting to help that person. A pastor friend of mine says we should consider principles above people and people above policy. Compassionate empathy involves working around policies when necessary to take care of others.

When my kids were little, I had a personal policy that I wouldn't take business meetings on Saturdays. Then enter Hector, a client who sold his software company for $1 million then used that money to purchase delivery vehicles and a warehouse to start a new company. Due to some improper planning, he soon found himself a million dollars in debt. That's when he began working with me. It had been about a year, and he was making great strides in getting back on track.

Early one particular Saturday morning as my family and I were heading out the door, I got an SOS call from Hector.

As soon as I heard his voice, I could tell he was struggling.

"I received some really bad news from my accountant," he said. "It doesn't look good, and I don't know what to do."

"What do you mean? What happened?"

"I knew it was bad, but things are much worse than I thought. I don't know if I can keep the doors open. I'm really scared."

"Try to calm down, everything is going to be okay," I said. "Tell me how I can help you."

"I just need someone to talk to."

"I can definitely meet with you on Monday, Hector."

"Okay," he said, but I could tell by the sound of his voice he wasn't okay, so I put the phone down and went to talk to my wife.

"Listen, I'm in a situation. Hector is in dire straits," I told her. "Would it be okay if we pushed everything to later in the morning, so I can meet him for breakfast?"

She said, "No problem. Go do what you have to do."

I got back on the phone with Hector and asked, "Can you meet me over at Bob Evans at 10 o'clock?"

"You mean this morning?"

"Yes."

"Is that alright? Am I interrupting family time?"

"Don't worry about it. I'll see you in a few minutes."

Keep in mind that it's one thing to have compassion and it's another thing to be compassionate. Being compassionate means exercising compassionate empathy. The meeting with Hector went well. In fact, about three months later he told me how much he appreciated me for taking the time to meet with him on that Saturday morning. He went on to explain how he believed that not only did our meeting save his business, but he believed it lifted him out of a dark place on a personal level.

Don't get me wrong, my first instinct wasn't to forgo that Saturday morning with my family to meet with a client. But over the years, I've learned the importance of making sacrifices. I've also learned that I can never understand the impact I can have on another individual's life until I get on the other side of empathy. For this reason and this reason alone, it's important that you're willing to work around your policies and rules, even modify your schedule, in an effort to take care of others.

Empathy Can't Be Forced

Empathy is important, but without internal motivation, it can backfire and work against you.

Think about all of those horrible customer service calls you've been forced to endure. How many times have you tried to call one of your 1-800 service providers and had to navigate through endless prompts before speaking to a real person? Finally, you get on the line with someone, and it's obvious they're reading from a script.

"I am so sorry to hear you're having a problem," the customer service representative says. "I am certainly happy to help you with this. So, how's your day going so far?"

How does this sequence of scripted questions make you feel? Do you feel like the so-called customer service representative on the other end of the phone really cares about you and how your day is going? No. Those calls can be extremely frustrating because it's obvious that the rep seems to care less about you and more about following the script. This is an example of someone trying to use empathy without internal motivation. It's inauthentic.

But every once in a while, you'll find yourself on the line with a customer service representative who cares more about you than the script.

You might say, "I'm getting frustrated after all those phone prompts, and now I have limited time."

Then you get a response like, "I'm with you. I'm sorry about all of those prompts. Let me put you on the fast track so you can get back to your day."

That representative gets it and isn't afraid to go off script to assist you because it's the right thing to do. That's empathy fueled by internal motivation, and you can see why it's much more effective.

Recognize Others' Emotions

Another RedRock Leadership training exercise involves me handing participants a notecard with one of four emotions written on it: fear, sadness, anger, and happiness. I have them pair up and give each person 30 seconds to silently act out the emotion to his or her partner. Most of the time, people get it right the first time.

Why is it so easy to recognize those emotions? One reason is because the exercise takes place in a closed environment where there are no distractions, and one person's entire focus is on the other person. It's interesting how you can identify another person's mood when you're focused solely on them.

Being able to recognize someone's mood or emotions during a training session can be somewhat challenging. However, the real challenge comes when you return to your world in real-time. Will you still be able to assess why someone (member of your team, boss, spouse, etc.) behaves a certain way? Problems arise when we jump to conclusions and react to someone else's behavior. This is what leads to a breach of integrity.

Let's say that someone at work misses a deadline and doesn't finish a project on time. How do you respond? If this is one of your stressors, then you're at risk of slipping into the Avoid State. When this happens, STAR and assume positive intent. Take the time to find out what prevented the person from completing the task.

When you find yourself successfully executing this way, you're improving in the areas of personal awareness, integrity, and internal motivation. The result is an increased ability to empathize. When this happens, those around you will be more likely to trust you and ask for help, which means they'll be less likely to miss another deadline.

CHAPTER 7

SOCIAL SKILLS

When we communicate, we typically fall into one of the following four categories:

1. **Assertive:** Straightforward, honest, caring, and reliable

2. **Aggressive:** Loud, angry, attacking, whining, guilt-inducing, manipulative

3. **Passive:** Timid, avoidant, tentative, non-responsive, frightened

4. **Passive-Aggressive:** Guilt-inducing, dishonest, underhanded, devious

Leaders are not aggressive, passive, or passive-aggressive. Leaders are assertive. Some of us are wired to be aggressive, and some of us are wired to be passive. Aggressive people are often quick to fight, and passive people are often quick to flee confrontation. It's that classic fight-or-flight pattern.

One of the greatest attributes of leaders is that they're assertive—meaning they're bold and confident in the way they communicate. Keep in mind that you can only be assertive if you're consciously tuned in to other people. Assertiveness is a highly developed social skill that helps you build positive relationships.

As motivational speaker Zig Ziglar says, "You can have everything in life you want if you will just help other people get what they want."

To be assertive, you must have enough margin in your life to be available to others, and you must have the desire to care. You have to speak up when something isn't right, even if it causes you to fall out of favor with certain people. When you're assertive at the right moments, then you're emotionally intelligent. If you find yourself being aggressive, passive, or passive-aggressive, it means that you're lacking in personal awareness, integrity, and internal motivation. Like I said, these skills are interconnected.

It's not easy to simply change our behavior or change our nature. It's common for people, both passive and aggressive types, to become passive-aggressive as they try to manage projects and take care of others. We all do. It's part of the human condition, but we must guard against this, starting with how we communicate.

How Do You Communicate?

The way you communicate often depends on your behavior style. You may enjoy small talk, but I may not. You may want details and facts, but I may feel my broad opinions will suffice. Identifying not only your own tendencies, but those of your team and close family members will help you open the lines of communication and better identify with your audience in any situation.

The method is just as important as the style of communication. Face-to-face and over-the-phone communication is slowly going away as we become more focused on doing business over instant messaging, email, text, and social media. Despite emerging trends, it's important to understand that if we're going to build positive relationships, face-to-face communication is the most effective method, with a telephone conversation or video call as the next best.

According to a study conducted by UCLA psychology professor Albert Mehrabian, when it comes to expressing our feelings and attitudes, 55 percent of the message is communicated through facial expressions or body language, while 38 percent is expressed through tone. Only 7 percent of the meaning of a message is communicated through verbal communication. Because phones (without video) make it impossible to convey facial expressions and body language, tone increases in importance from 38 percent to 84 percent, while the significance of our words increases from 7 percent to 16 percent.[6]

Regardless of the medium you choose, you'll be most effective when you communicate assertively. To do this, make a conscious effort to remain in the Approach State because it's virtually impossible to control your tone, non-verbal cues, or your words if you're in the Avoid State.

As my pastor friend says, "What's down in the well comes up in the bucket."

This means whatever we feel inside will show in our communications, whether verbally or through tonality and body language in the form of gestures, facial expressions, posture, etc. Also, what comes out through our mouths typically reflects what's in our hearts. We

6 https://arlenetaylor.org/communication-and-the-brain/3147-mehrabian-communication-research

need to view ourselves the way others do and understand how they receive our message.

If you aren't sure how you come across when you communicate, record yourself or ask someone else to record you while you interact with others or deliver a presentation. It will be an eye-opening experience because you'll recognize things about yourself, good and not so good, that will help you improve the way you communicate.

The DISC Behavior Language

DISC measures the four dimensions of normal behavior (Dominance, Influence, Steadiness, and Compliance). Once we understand DISC, we can assess individual action preferences to predict how we behave in particular situations.

RedRock Leadership is a Value-Added Associate for TTI Success Insights, an assessment company headquartered in Scottsdale, Arizona. There's a lot I like about TTI. For starters, as the first company to put the DISC behavior language into a customized written report, they have helped more than 100,000 companies in 115 countries with more than 30 million individual assessments in 47 languages. In addition, they've been awarded four US patents, including one for brain research. The reliability of TTI's assessments is second to none.

If you're interested in a deeper understanding of your behaviors (DISC), go to RedRockLeadership.com/the-book for more information about how to receive a personalized TTI Talent Insights° DISC assessment. There is also information there about how to become certified in the DISC behavior language.

One of the more fascinating aspects of this assessment is a section called "perceptions." The section is broken down into three segments:

1.   How you see yourself

2.   How others see you when you're under moderate stress

3.   How others see you when you're under extreme stress

Rarely does anyone disagree with the first part because it includes a lot of positive traits, but some people adamantly deny what's written about them in the second and third sections. That's understandable because when we're under moderate or extreme stress, our personal awareness is lower. In reality, people rarely ever see themselves as others see them. Gaining that knowledge, even if it comes in the form of hard truths, makes the DISC assessment extremely useful. It forces you to come to terms with your behavior and figure out how to leverage your strengths.

What Is DISC?

The earliest form of behavior studies can be traced all the way back to about 370 B.C. to Greek physician Hippocrates and his concept of differing temperaments. His four observed temperaments were described as "sanguine," "choleric," "melancholic," and "phlegmatic."

In 1921, Swiss psychiatrist Carl Jung further formulated the temperaments into four psychological functions he called "thinking," "feeling," "sensation," and "intuition." Then, in 1928, a Harvard-educated PhD by the name of William Moulton Marston published the book *Emotions of Normal People*, which developed into what we know today as DISC.

Marston was a contributing writer to the *American Journal of Psychology, Encyclopedia Britannica,* and the *Encyclopedia of Psychology.* He also created the superhero Wonder Woman. One of his most prolific contributions to society was the lie detector. After working with several thousand criminals in Texas, his test was found to be 97 percent reliable. Marston noted that his test wasn't applicable only to criminal psychology, but also was useful in determining other social and psychological issues.

He defined the four dimensions of normal behavior (DISC) as:

> **D**ominance: How you respond to problems and challenges
>
> **I**nfluence: How you influence others to your point of view
>
> **S**teadiness: How you respond to the pace of your environment
>
> **C**ompliance: How you respond to rules and procedures set by others

Marston also described these as predictable traits that we act out in our everyday lives. He saw DISC behavior styles as both internal and innate but also impacted largely by our external environment. Let's take a closer look at them.

People characterized by highly dominant behavior are intently focused and act with purpose. They don't waste any steps or time doing whatever it is they need to get done. They take charge and make decisions quickly, even if that means trusting their gut without having all the necessary information. They're risk takers who strive to make things happen. Their hobbies often include competitive sports.

To communicate effectively with someone who has this behavior style, you want to have all the facts and make your point quickly. They don't want to hear problems without ideas for potential solutions. Avoid small talk or long emails. Be aware that those with a high D factor fear being taken advantage of, and their response to stress is expressed through anger.

Individuals with a high influence dimension to their behavior love people. They are social and talkative. Their world revolves around people, and they feel most energized when they're around others. They often carry around pictures of their family and friends and don't want to be isolated or work alone. They have the ability to make others feel comfortable and tend to have a positive, optimistic attitude. Outside of work, these individuals tend to enjoy social events and traveling.

To communicate with someone like this, you simply need to start a conversation, if they don't beat you to it. It doesn't always matter what you talk about. And remember that eye contact makes them happy. Recognize that their greatest fear is social rejection, and their response to stress is expressed through optimism.

People whose behavior is marked by high steadiness are all about loyalty, and that loyalty extends to just about everything—people, stores, routines and procedures. They feel that slow and steady wins the race. They don't get too high or too low and strive to keep an even keel. They tend to like people but not in the same way as an influencer. They have no problem letting a dominant or influential person take the spotlight. Outside of work, a person with a high S factor will typically find enjoyment in activities like yard work or spending time with their family.

When communicating with them, it's all about maintaining a steady demeanor and pace. Don't come on too strong or you risk making them feel uneasy. They fear change and the loss of security, and their response to stress is expressed through a blank expression, without showing any emotion.

People who score high in terms of compliant behavior thrive on rules and accurate information. They observe the rules of society because they trust those rules were created for a reason. They have high standards for both themselves and others. They tend to have task-oriented hobbies like puzzles or DIY projects and rarely waste time getting to work. At times, they can seem pessimistic because of their belief that anything that can go wrong will go wrong.

Communicating with a highly compliant individual can be difficult because they're not natural conversationalists and don't necessarily like idle chit-chat or small talk. They want details and facts because they don't like indecision or gray areas and want a complete picture of the situation at hand. Recognize that they have a fear of the unknown, and their response to stress is expressed through worry.

It's also worth taking a look at the areas where you don't score high in DISC. This knowledge provides insight into how to prepare and navigate activities and conversations for which you may not be adequately equipped.

For example, people with low dominance scores will be challenged in an environment where they're expected to respond and fix problems quickly with little or no guidance or information. Those with low influence scores will feel uncomfortable in a highly social environment. Those with low steadiness scores will feel undue pressure when they're told what to do and how to do it, and individuals with low compliant scores won't function well in a highly regulated environment with strict standards and other operating requirements. This knowledge can help you understand when you'll need the necessary energy to adapt, step away, or lean on others who complement your individual behavior style.

To illustrate the differences in these behavior styles during RedRock Leadership training sessions, I ask participants to picture themselves inside a room with the doors sealed shut and the windows made of unbreakable glass. Suddenly, the fire alarm goes off, and we can see smoke coming from under the door. We're all stuck inside the room. How would everyone react?

I explain that dominant individuals will run around, demanding to know who set the fire, while those with a high influence factor may deny there's a fire and tell everyone not to worry. Even if there is a fire, they believe that the fire department will arrive soon and put it out.

People known for steady behavior silently huddle together under a desk, each with just a single tear running down their cheek, while those who are highly compliant make it clear that they knew something like this was going to happen. Their thinking is along the lines of, "I was worried when I woke up this morning that I might not make it through the day alive."

If you're wondering why no one tried to get out of the room, that's a good question—but this illustration is an exaggeration to prove a point. I've yet to have anyone tell me that they disagree with what this depicts about themselves and what they know of how others behave when under extreme stress. The high D's are angry and demanding. The high I's are optimistic to the point of being unrealistic and annoying. The high S's hold everything inside and appear unemotional, while the high C's worry.

To further drive my point home during RedRock Leadership training, I ask participants to get into groups and create posters for their particular behavior styles. I also ask them to work together to choose the car they would drive and the music they would play. The results are predictable: The D's pick a song like "Eye of the Tiger" and drive a Ferrari while the I's choose a song like "Party in the U.S.A." to go with a Mustang Convertible. The high S's pick a song like "I'll Be There for You" to go along with a Chevy or Ford Pickup, and the C's select a song like "Tell Me Why" and drive a Suburban or Explorer. It's really interesting to see how people with the same behavior styles tend to have similar tastes. It's even more interesting to listen to their tone of voice and watch their body language when they explain how and why they made their selections. This exercise is particularly helpful to those who are learning to identify the behavior styles of others.

At this point, it's important to note that the TTI Talent Insights behavioral assessment is not a personality test. It's used to create win-win relationships, and it's not meant to give anyone ideas for manipulating others. In addition, there are no right answers, and no one behavior style is better than another. Each style is a combination of all four factors, and adaptation to any style is possible with effort and awareness. We find that when a team learns the DISC behavior language, their communication improves, and their culture gets stronger.

Communicating with Others

When you're learning a language, it's always good to have resources that can better help you understand yourself and others. We have many downloadable materials at RedRockLeadership.com/the-book, including the RedRock Leadership Toolbox with a RedRock Relationship Reference Card,™ and the RedRock Social Style Battlecards.™

We break down the communication tips by occupation so whether you're a salesperson, manager, administrator, or executive, you can learn how to most effectively communicate with people who have different jobs and behavior styles.

I also use a RedRock Leadership training exercise called "Coach Them Up" to help individuals improve their communication skills. To get started, I place participants into groups based on similar behavior styles. I have them refer to the RedRock Relationship Reference Card and the checklist for communicating that appears in each of their personal assessments. Next, I ask them to select one person to play the role of a struggling team member and another to play the role of a manager, while the others observe.

The objective of this training exercise is for the manager to coach the struggling team member back to his or her higher level of productivity and performance, using the following background information:

1. A new team member was paired with an experienced team member during their first 30 days with the company.

2. Following the initial training, this new team member demonstrated determination and initiative.

3. The new team member has been on board for nearly 90 days. Individual momentum has slowed, and personal productivity has dropped.

The first part of this exercise runs fairly smooth, and when I ask everyone how it went, they tell me it was easy. Some even say they feel like they just met their kindred spirit.

What the group doesn't realize is that I'm about to mix them up and have them run through the same exercise with people who have different behavior styles. The next round doesn't typically go as well and usually results in a lot of stress. People rarely pay much attention to the RedRock Relationship Reference Card nor the checklist for communicating in the second round. Why is that?

One reason is because they don't leave their comfort zones. Things went so well during the first round that they didn't think about using new communication tools in the second round. This is exactly what happens in real life, isn't it? Only in real life, when we treat people how we want to be treated instead of how they want to be treated, the interpersonal conflict has deeper consequences.

Think about it. If you're a compliant person and I'm an influencer, my way of communicating will involve trying to influence you and get you to like me. But if you're a compliant person, you're more focused on obtaining facts and details than you are about making a friend.

Understand Your Adapted Style and Natural Style

All of us have both adapted and natural behavior styles, and the assessment we use during RedRock Leadership training sheds light on how we behave with each style.

> **Adapted Behavior Style**: This is our "game face." It's our conscious behavior based on the present. It's also the most changeable style, and it tends to be the way we behave at work.

> **Natural Behavior Style:** This is our gut reaction, or our unconscious behavior. It's based on past experiences, and it's the least changeable. This is who we are when we're stressed or at rest.

When I meet you for the first time, you will see my game face. Once we have a comfortable relationship, I'll be more likely to move into what's called my natural style.

The key to all of this is twofold: First and foremost, recognize your own behavior style and the value you bring to relationships. Second, recognize the behavior styles of other people so you can respond in a manner that makes them feel most comfortable and builds positive relationships.

Where this gets really interesting is how close together, or far apart, an adapted style is from a natural style. For some people, there isn't a lot of difference between the two, and for others, their adapted and natural styles are completely different. When a person's natural and adapted styles are close together, you will see little difference, if any at all, between who they are at home and who they are at work.

When a person's natural and adapted styles are further apart, there will be noticeable differences between home and work behaviors.

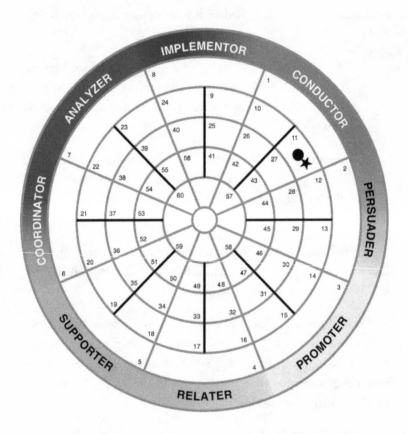

Let's look at how adapted and natural behavior styles play out for William, the operations manager Craig hired at J-TEK. (In the illustration, the star marks his adapted style and the dot represents his natural style.)

I introduced William to Craig because I thought he would be a good fit for his company. Craig hired him, and everything seemed to be going well. Three weeks later, I received a call.

"We've got a problem," Craig said. "William is flipping people off and using really bad language. That doesn't fly around here, and it's starting to offend some people.

"Really? That doesn't sound like the William I know."

I approached William and told him we were getting some complaints.

"What gives?" I asked him.

"I'm not mad, and I don't mean anything by it," he said. "I flip people off and drop f-bombs all the time. It's just who I am."

The three of us looked at William's assessment. We saw that the star and the dot representing his adapted and natural behavior styles were virtually on top of each other. I explained to Craig how that meant William behaved the same way, regardless of where he was or what he was doing—in sum, he lacked personal awareness.

Once it was brought to his attention, William committed to adjusting how he communicated with the team. Craig was satisfied with William's commitment. They shook hands and moved forward. This could have been a situation that caused major stress and conflict, but it was easily resolved once both parties understood William's behavior style.

Challenges arise when adapted and natural styles are close together, but the opposing scenario (when they are far apart) can lead to another set of issues. One major problem occurs when people get stressed and shift into their natural style. Since it's so different from their adapted style, it can lead to severe embarrassment or frustration and take a long time for them to recover.

This is another reason why it's important to condition ourselves to be aware of our stressors and manage our emotions accordingly.

Task and People Orientation / Introverts and Extroverts

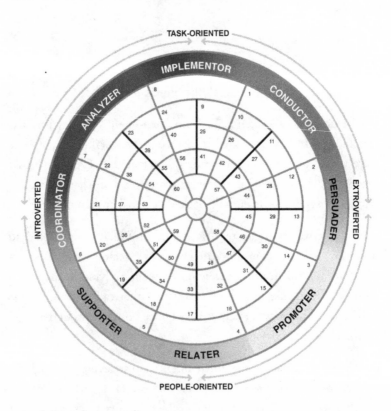

A few other ways to better understand ourselves and others is to know the main differences between task- and people-orientation as well as introverts and extroverts. In this illustration, task-oriented people reside in the top two quadrants, and people-oriented people reside in the bottom two quadrants. Introverts occupy the two quadrants on the left side of the wheel, and extroverts occupy the two quadrants on the right side.

Generally speaking, here are the common traits of an individual who is task-oriented:[7]

- Focuses on completing the project at hand
- Sets goals and clear paths to complete objectives
- Operates by schedules and deadlines
- Is more structured than not
- Wants roles and goals
- Is tuned in to producing desired results

Generally speaking, here are the common traits of someone who is people-oriented:

- Focuses on satisfaction, motivation, and well-being of others
- Facilitates positive and productive interaction between other members of the team
- Less structured
- Desires teamwork and clear communication
- Interested in team-building meetings and exercises

7 https://www.eskill.com/blog/task-people-oriented-management/

Here are common traits of an introvert:[8]

- Enjoys spending time in solitude
- Prefers not to be the center of attention
- Values close one-on-one relationships
- Thinks before they speak
- Needs time alone to recharge and reflect
- Prefers working in quiet, independent environments
- Is deeply focused and thinks about specific interests
- Can be seen as reserved

Here are common traits of an extrovert:[9]

- Enjoys being the center of attention
- Has large social networks
- Tends to think out loud
- Makes quick decisions
- Gains energy from being around other people
- Is outgoing, enthusiastic, and positive
- Thrives in team-oriented and open work settings

I work with a pair of business owners who are husband and wife. He's a task-oriented extrovert, and she's a task-oriented introvert. He's continually frustrated because she tends to hold back and not offer her opinions. She says that when she does offer her opinions, he cuts her off and doesn't listen to her point of view. He says she's negative and overly cautious; she says he's unrealistic and reckless. Because he tends to talk louder and faster than her, I've coached him and helped him understand that their relationship would improve if he'd just wait for her to speak and actively listen to her.

8 https://www.prevention.com/health/mental-health/a24068521/introvert-vs-extrovert/
9 https://www.prevention.com/health/mental-health/a24068521/introvert-vs-extrovert/

I personally believe the extrovert in any relationship, personal or professional, carries the weight of the responsibility for setting the tone for productive and proactive communication. Whenever someone learns to speak less and listen more, he or she always benefits. Introverts actually have the advantage here as they tend to be better listeners.[10] They just need to become more comfortable speaking up.

It can be easy for an extrovert to jump to conclusions and say their introverted counterparts are fueled by insecurities. The same could actually be said about an extrovert who doesn't stop talking. I know because I'm an extrovert, and when I'm insecure or under stress and my personal awareness is diminished, I tend to begin filling in all the blanks and then some. When I'm under stress, I literally don't know when to stop talking. I just keep going and going and going. One day, a friend tactfully pointed out that I was dominating the conversation and sucking all of the oxygen out of the room.

It has taken me many years to learn silence is golden. When I manage my emotions, I'm in a much better position to listen intently to what other people are saying, especially when I don't agree with them. As I focus my attention on the conversation, I find myself engaged and asking questions. As a result I actually become invested and interested in the conversation.

Similarly, I worked with an introverted executive client who expressed her frustrations about not contributing at a level congruent with her ability or desire. She'd tell me about sitting in meetings wanting to speak up but feeling daunted by the thought of "competing with strong personalities in the room."

---

10 https://time.com/5373403/surprising-benefits-introvert/

"When that happens, I feel conflicted because I feel like I don't have anything to say even though I want to say something," she told me. "So, I just sit there feeling frustrated."

We worked together, and I helped her learn how to be bolder and more confident and how to speak to be heard, without backing down. As she made progress, she was able to pinpoint and understand the insecurities and stress that caused her personal awareness to diminish. This was huge for her because it answered the question she could never seem to answer: Why am I always on the outside of a conversation, looking in?

It took some time for her to learn to speak up quickly with confidence, but eventually she did. As she learned to manage her emotions, she was able to offer a greater contribution in more and more meetings. I've seen positive results from the training and coaching I've provided to introverts like her. (If you want more information on how to be perceived as bolder and more confident, check out our resources at RedRockLeadership.com/the-book.)

Every behavior style has its strengths and its weaknesses. The challenge is being able to recognize your nature for what it really is, to understand how insecurity can manifest itself, and to find a balance instead of doing just what's easy or natural.

CHAPTER 8

12 DRIVING FORCES™

It isn't always easy to engage people in work that is personally meaningful to them. Even if you're able to do this, you still have to be effective in communicating your organizations value to them in ways they prefer. But how do you identify specifically what motivates each person in your organization?

It's the right culture that allows a person to be motivated and stay motivated. Every decision we make is made in accordance with our individual motivators such as our personal interests, attitudes, and core values. To better understand a person's motivation, we must take a look at their 12 Driving Forces.™ So what exactly are these 12 Driving Forces?

After more than 30 years of studying human behavior and motivation, PhD scientists at TTI have identified the following 12 Driving Forces. One of the main reasons why RedRock Leadership partners with TTI Success Insights is because they add dimension to their assessments by integrating an individual's behaviors (DISC) with their 12 Driving Forces, in a dual science assessment.

The history of 12 Driving Forces begins with German psychologist Eduard Spranger. His work was first translated in 1928 in *Types of Men*. Spranger's work led to the creation of six categories that focused on an individual's drivers, or "why" they do what they do. His work was followed by the Allport-Vernon Study of Values, a questionnaire published in 1931 that measured individual values on the basis of declared personal preferences.

In recent years, TTI, led by Bill Bonnstetter, developed its own assessment in the 1990s based on the Study of Values. The assessment was revised to its final form in early 2015. If you're interested in a deeper level understanding of your 12 Driving Forces, go to RedRockLeadership.com/the-book for more information about receiving your personalized assessment. There is also information there about how to become certified in the 12 Driving Forces.

Think of it like this: Your driving forces represent your personal interests, individual attitude, and what you value most. While DISC, or your behaviors, represent "how" you do what you do, your driving forces represent "why" you do what you do. In the TTI Talent Insights assessment, 12 Driving Forces are measured based on Spranger's six original categories.

Each category represents a continuum with a Driving Force at each end:

Instinctive	Knowledge	Intellectual
Selfless	Utility	Resourceful
Objective	Surroundings	Harmonious
Intentional	People	Altruistic
Collaborative	Power	Commanding
Receptive	Methodologies	Structured

To put this another way:

- Motives for obtaining information (knowledge) range from instinctive to intellectual.

- Motives for accomplishing tasks or projects (utility) range from selfless to resourceful.

- Motives for tolerating or controlling the surrounding environment (surroundings) range from objective to harmonious.

- Motives for dealing with people (others) range from intentional to altruistic.

- Motives for status and recognition (power) range from collaboration to commanding.

- Motives for adhering to proven or less proven strategies (methodologies) range from receptive to structured.

Let's explore these motivations in greater depth:

Knowledge (Instinctive to Intellectual)

Instinctive people love to apply what they have learned. They're interested in learning more about how to accomplish tasks at hand, particularly if they can learn by doing. They get a lot out of being mentored and are motivated by using their past knowledge and experience because they want to apply it for mutual gain.

An intellectual person is driven by opportunities to continue learning. They're motivated to understand all the available knowledge on just about any subject. A person with a high intellectual driving force enjoys the opportunity to solve problems and discover new information.

Personally, I'm instinctive (an experiential learner) who's not motivated to read instructions before diving into something new—it's just not important to me to gain knowledge before I start a project. On the flip side, intellectual people appreciate having clear instructions and directions because it's important for them to be knowledgeable before they get involved with a project. That doesn't necessarily mean they analyze things (that's more of a behavior style); it means that they have a stronger desire to obtain information before they step into action. In other words, they want to know all there is to know about a project before they get involved.

Utility (Selfless to Resourceful)

Selfless people are driven to complete tasks and projects for the greater good. It's more important to them to achieve something for the sake of accomplishment, rather than to get something in return. Individuals with a selfless driving force thrive on being a team player rather than a catalyst for action. These people like opportunities that will allow them to be part of a cohesive team that gets results.

Resourceful people are driven to experience a high return on investment for their time, talent, and money. They are high achievers who enjoy being challenged. Those with a high resource driving force are motivated by opportunities to apply their time, talent, energy, and resources to achieve significant results.

I once worked with a woman named Sharon, who held an important role as a permit coordinator for a construction company that was a highly resourceful emerging growth company. Her job was to obtain permits for all their new jobs, but those located at the city office who were in charge of permitting would typically take their time. They'd tell Sharon the permit would be ready by the end of the week. But it would get delayed week after week, and she wasn't motivated to push the envelope to speed things up.

Every time this happened, the owner would go ballistic because his company couldn't begin jobs without permits. Because he is resourceful, he introduced a reward system that he thought would personally motivate Sharon to help speed up the permitting process. However, the reward system didn't work because Sharon didn't appreciate it. She's selfless and driven to complete tasks with little to no expectation of receiving anything in return. The owner's reward system was counterproductive, and unfortunately, Sharon ended up leaving his company.

It's unfortunate because Sharon was a good worker. She wasn't any less interested in making sure jobs got permits than the owner was. What's even more unfortunate is that the owner will continue to have this problem unless he hires someone with a high resourceful/low selfless driver or learns how to communicate effectively with those who have high selfless/low resourceful drivers.

Surroundings (Objective to Harmonious)

Objective people are driven by the functionality of their surroundings. They make decisions based on facts and logic and prefer function over form. They don't appreciate when there's drama going on around them. They're not motivated by luxurious offices and can thrive in the midst of difficult circumstances. They like opportunities to achieve desired, logical outcomes.

Harmonious individuals are artistic, emotional, and subjective thinkers. They enjoy the experience involved with beautifying the world around them. The enjoy harmony and balance in their relationships. They're motivated by a nice, clean, and tidy work space. Harmonious people like opportunities to be creative and develop positive, personal relationships.

Others (Intentional to Altruistic)

Intentional people are driven to assist others when their own interests align with a specific purpose of others, not just for the sake of being helpful or supportive. They're the "nothing personal, it's strictly business" type. They appreciate others who can help them achieve their goals.

Altruistic people want to make the world a better place by eliminating conflict. They have a deep desire to help people; they like using their time, talents, and resources to help and support others. They appreciate being involved in opportunities to apply their ideas for the benefit of others.

Consider the case of Abby, an HR director who called me in to provide RedRock Leadership training for one of her teams. As it turned out, I'm objective and she's harmonious. This led to some minor conflict as soon as we started working together.

I created detailed slides to provide participants with what they needed to learn. She worried that some of my slides weren't easy enough for participants to understand. I wanted to arrange the chairs in a U-shape for maximum learning efficiency, and she wanted round tables so her team felt more comfortable. I suggested 10-minute breaks so that people could take a breather, and she thought her team needed 20 minutes to decompress before re-engaging. I didn't want any cell phones or computers on the tables because participants would be distracted, and she felt like we would hurt their feelings if we told them they couldn't remain connected to the outside world.

Neither one of us cared any more or any less about the people who would engage in the training. It's just that she is altruistic and I'm intentional. Once we took the time to understand each other's perspectives, we were able to collaborate and compromise to create a more productive and dynamic experience for the training participants—a win-win outcome!

Power (Collaborative to Commanding)

Collaborative people are driven to play a supporting role within an organization with little need for individual recognition. They're not motivated by titles or contests that pit people against each other. These people want opportunities to work on a team where they can help support others in accomplishing their goals.

Commanding people desire control and opportunities to advance in their careers. These people like status and authority, and they appreciate the ability to assert control over others' futures. They also appreciate personal recognition. They desire the opportunity to be in a leadership role where they can plan and execute a winning strategy.

Methodologies (Receptive to Structured)

Receptive people are motivated by using more than one method to get things done. They enjoy finding alternatives to the status quo. When making decisions, they appreciate the opportunity to consider a variety of options. They like to experiment "outside the box" and come up with different approaches to identify and create new ways of achieving results.

Structured people are motivated by using traditional methods to get results. These people see one way of doing things, which they refer to as the "right" way. They appreciate proven methods and will implement systems to get things done right the first time. These people tend to be religious about the critical aspects of their lives such as their health and spirituality. Structured people like to rely upon proven methods to achieve results.

The integration of 12 Driving Forces and DISC adds a whole new dimension to our understanding of ourselves and of others. For example, one of my primary driving forces is structure, and one of my primary behavior factors is dominance (D). When I'm asked to consider looking at different ways of doing things, I can appear obstinate, closed-minded, and even inflexible. However, my high D behavior factor indicates that I'm pioneering and ambitious. Internally, I will fight to hold on to what I consider to be a proven method, while externally I want to charge ahead toward something new and great.

With more insight into what motivates me, I'm learning how to stop, breathe, and allow other people to speak while I listen. Then, I can use what I've learned to fuel my pioneering behavior style. Needless to say, this level of personal awareness has been incredibly liberating for me!

By not taking such a firm position, I'm able to adapt. Still, there will always be situations that will require more energy than I have in the time available. When that happens, I must walk away, STAR, and return once I'm no longer in danger of falling prey to one of my stressors.

The TTI Talent Insight assessment used in RedRock Leadership training breaks down the 12 Driving Forces into three clusters to help participants gain a deeper understanding of what actually drives them into action. Keep in mind that the higher the driving force score is, the more passionate someone is in that area. The higher scores make up what's called the primary driving forces cluster. The lower the scores, the more indifferent someone is to those forces.

Here is a breakdown of the three clusters:

1. **Primary Driving Forces.** Your top driving forces create a cluster of drivers that move you to action. If you focus on the cluster rather than a single driver, you can create combinations that provide a deeper level of understanding about what motivates you. For example, if your primary driving forces cluster are commanding, objective, intellectual, and intentional, you will thrive in a culture where you are singled out and recognized for your accomplishments. You will also desire to be in a practical, no-nonsense work environment where you have plenty of time to research and obtain knowledge before having to take action. Finally, you want the opportunity to help people for a specific purpose such as increasing company sales, gaining market share, or improving customer service.

2. **Situational Driving Forces.** Your mid-level driving forces create a cluster of drivers that come into play on a situational basis after your primary drivers are satisfied. For example, if your situational driving forces are receptive, selfless, resourceful, and structured and your primary driving forces have been satisfied, you'll be open to investigating new methods and ideas. In addition, you'll be motivated to

complete tasks without being held to deadlines or specific completion dates; you'll also be motivated to attain practical results that benefit you personally. Finally, you'll want to lean on proven methods for future results.

3. **Indifferent Driving Forces.** You may feel indifferent toward some or all of the drivers in this cluster. In fact, they could actually cause adverse reactions. For example, if your indifferent driving forces include altruistic, harmonious, instinctive and collaborative, you may be resistant to a culture that requires you to gain satisfaction from assisting people for the sole purpose of being helpful or supportive. In addition, you may lack motivation in a work environment where you are required to always be neat and tidy with a leadership team who expects you to rely upon intuition and jump into action without investigation or research. Your feeling of discomfort could get even worse if you're asked to do this from a supporting role without any public recognition or opportunity for advancement.

Having a better understanding of your 12 Driving Forces will help you improve your personal awareness, which will prevent you from slipping into the Avoid State. It will also help you understand how others perceive you.

During RedRock Leadership training, we use information in the TTI Talent Insights assessments to establish realistic expectations for you and your team. When you are able to anticipate issues and problems, you can get in front of them with coaching. Coaching will help minimize frustrations by managing expectations of your culture.

Have you ever seen someone struggling to get out of the Avoid State? If you have, then you would have noticed their negative attitude. In most cases, this is a direct result of their driving forces not being satisfied by the environment and culture that surrounds them.

I have a client who is a pilot. While going through RedRock Leadership training, he told me his assessment reminded him of when he flew his private plane through an ice storm. He was taught to trust his instruments, stay the course, and not panic. The worst thing he could do was ramp up his engines or change his elevation because he would find himself in a dangerous situation. He learned that if he didn't panic, he'd eventually make it out of the storm. Similarly, when times are tough, we don't know how long we'll need to endure them. But we know they will eventually come to pass. The TTI Talent Insights assessment is an instrument to guide you through tough times and help you stay the course.

Understanding your 12 Driving Forces will also help you learn to manage expectations and persevere in a culture or environment filled with stressors. If done successfully, you'll enhance your culture, create diversity, and build an environment of trust where a higher level of emotional intelligence exists.

After attending RedRock Leadership training, many clients tell me they never thought it was possible for them to appreciate and forge certain relationships. I've had architects and engineers say they never thought they'd build such positive connections with salespeople, and vice versa. But RedRock Leadership training gave them the tools they needed to forge win-win relationships. It's also helped people understand their past professional failures and successes and improve their personal relationships at home.

CHAPTER 9

MOTIVATE YOUR TEAM

I am often asked this question: "How can I motivate my people?" The answer may surprise you. The only productive long-term solution to motivating people is to create a culture where people can motivate themselves.

Too many organizations attempt to improve motivation and increase engagement levels by dangling carrots just out of reach to get people to do more. They also use the proverbial stick to poke them when they fall behind. This is called the carrot-and-stick method, an antiquated approach that actually produces diminishing returns.

Attitude determines motivation, but what shapes someone's attitude? It's gratitude. The root cause of frustration is missed expectations, and this leads people to be less appreciative. Of course, those who are unappreciative lack gratitude, and where there is a lack of gratitude, you'll find a negative attitude. When you find someone with a negative attitude, look closely, and you'll also notice they lack motivation.

For someone like me, a recovering perfectionist who sees everything in black-and-white, it can be challenging to be grateful in every situation. My expectations tend to be so high that it's nearly impossible to make it through a day and not be frustrated. Some years ago, I was fortunate to have a coach help me understand my 12 Driving Forces and how I was wired. He helped me understand my tendencies and taught me strategies for lowering my expectations to make way for gratitude. This is why it's a good idea to have a coach and to coach your people. The right kind of coaching will help clear mind "trash" and reprogram positive thinking.

In business, we deal with coworkers and customers, along with countless other people, problems, and issues on a daily basis. One way to rise up against the many challenges we face is to keep a daily gratitude journal. Give it a shot! It takes less than 10 minutes a day to write down 10 things for which you're grateful. It's a great way to stay motivated.

Set Yourself Up for Success

Gratitude is one part of the equation. The second is character. Character can be defined as what you do when others aren't looking. When you're aligned with your company's core values, you have a greater likelihood of improving your personal awareness, integrity, and internal motivation.

This is why it's important to bring people on to your team who align with the company values. If you don't, you run the risk of exposing their character flaws. Some people have very strong beliefs. If you hire someone who doesn't value what your organization stands for, he or she will be less motivated to trust and follow you in the direction you lead him or her.

Years ago, owners could lay out the way they wanted their organizations to be run and tell their team members to check their egos at the door. This type of strategy isn't effective anymore. If your core values aren't at the forefront of everything you do, your culture will suffer and you'll ultimately set yourself and your organization up for failure.

Certain organizations are run by people who have high expectations for how their customers will be treated or how quickly things must get done. Other organizations place greater emphasis on working and playing together as a team. Just because your core values are not visibly posted doesn't mean you don't have them. Make your core values and expectations clear to your entire team, and you'll solidify your culture by creating an environment of trust. During RedRock Leadership training, someone always asks, "What happens if I can't get people who are an exact match for my culture?"

Look, I get it. It's challenging enough to find someone to work the front desk, let alone a very specific high-tech position. The labor pool might be limited, and there's a chance your core values might limit options even further. Sometimes you just want a warm body, but you have to be realistic when it comes to the bigger picture. You can't be a fast-moving person who wants to go all the time and expect a bunch of laid-back individuals to fit into your culture.

I'm not saying you shouldn't hire people just because they don't meet your core values right out of the gate. Once you have those core values outlined, you can have a discussion with potential team members about your expectations. You might be surprised at the number of people who are willing to adhere to your core values once you spell them out. It's worse if you hire someone and later learn that he or she isn't willing or able to adhere to them.

The point isn't to hire or work with people who are exactly like you. That's impossible. People don't have to be just like you in order to buy in. But keep in mind that leaders don't push people, they lead people. A friend of mine always says be a lighthouse, not a tugboat—I love that! Things move fast today and you don't want people lagging behind. You must surround yourself with people who are motivated and empowered to support your culture.

The RedRock Core-Valuator™

I'm a strong proponent of creating an environment characterized by collaboration and trust. As a leader, it's your job to not only build this type of environment but to protect it. During RedRock Leadership training, we introduce the RedRock Core-Valuator." This is a tool that allows you to assess each member of your team against your stated and defined core values. It will help you determine where there are needs for coaching and harnessing harmful behavior.

You can download the RedRock Core-Valuator at RedRock Leadership.com/the-book.

Here is how to use the RedRock Core-Valuator.

1. Enter the names of each of the members of your team in the column on the left.

2. Enter your stated core values across the top.

3. Using the scale, rate each team member on how often he or she complies with your stated core values. Enter the scores into the grid.

RedRock Core-Valuator™

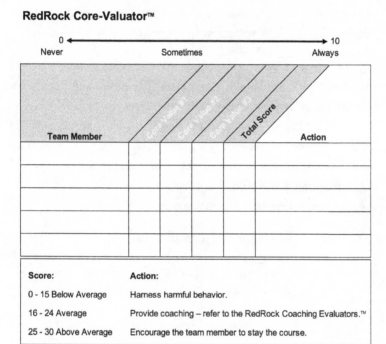

Score:	Action:
0 - 15 Below Average	Harness harmful behavior.
16 - 24 Average	Provide coaching – refer to the RedRock Coaching Evaluators.™
25 - 30 Above Average	Encourage the team member to stay the course.

Harnessing Harmful Behavior

We've all had that moment when we spotted the apple in the fruit bowl starting to go bad. At first, there's a small brown spot, but you leave it alone. The next day, you realize that the brown spot is a little bigger, but you don't throw it out. On the third day, it becomes clear that the rotten apple is contaminating other fruit in the bowl.

I'm sure you see where I'm going with this. To protect your culture and build an environment of trust, you must deal with the "rotting apples." You can do this by harnessing harmful behavior.

Let's say Steve is a rotting apple who scored less than a 16 on your RedRock Core-Valuator. You must take action and harness his harmful behavior. That doesn't mean there has to be a harsh conversation. Instead, you're going to sit down with him, assume positive intent, and take an approach geared toward helping him get back on track. That being said, it's important to have an exit strategy worked out before you begin. Finally, when you enter this discussion, be sure that you're prepared to remain in the Approach State.

Here are the steps to harness harmful behavior:

1.   Inform your team member of inconsistencies between his or her actions and your organization's core values.

2.   State the consequences of these inconsistencies.

3.   Invite him or her to discuss the issues and listen to his or her comments.

4.   Review expectations about course correction.

5.   Ask for a commitment to improve.

6.   If there is a commitment to improve, express appreciation and establish a timeline to follow up.

7.   If there is not a commitment to improve, discuss an exit strategy.

Let me give you a sample script:

First, call Steve into the office, conference room, or a location where you are both comfortable. Start by building him up to give him a little lift.

YOU: Steve, I want to let you know I thoroughly appreciate everything you do. That said, there are a few inconsistencies that we need to talk about.

STEVE: Oh, okay. What's wrong?

YOU: I'm observing that your actions aren't always in line with two of our team's core values: prepared and diligent. I just think we need to address them for you and for us.

STEVE: I'm not sure that I know what you're talking about. I've worked here for years, and nobody has said anything about this before.

YOU: Fair enough. I want you to know that the only reason I'm bringing this to your attention is because I care. I think you can be more prepared and diligent. If you don't improve in these areas, it can lead to issues down the line that can hinder your growth as an individual and the company as a whole.

STEVE: I thought I was prepared and diligent. Has someone complained?

YOU: We want to catch it before someone else does, so let's talk about expectations and course correction. First off, I notice that you've been coming in late, so can you focus on getting here 15 minutes earlier every morning? And when you attend our morning huddles, be sure to bring a notebook and pen to the meeting and detailed notes about your daily action items. Finally, make it a point to call in at the end of every day and report your hours to Margie so we can get invoices out on time.

STEVE: Is there anything else?

YOU: No, that's it. Can I get your commitment to improve in those areas, so you can be more prepared and diligent throughout the week?

STEVE: Yes. I can do that.

YOU: I'm excited that you want to make those improvements, and I'm all in with you. I want to set up a checkpoint in two weeks to see how things are going and to make sure that we're on the same page. I trust you and believe that you're committed to change. I'm here to support you in any way, so let's get going.

Keep in mind that this is an abbreviated and optimal version of this conversation. It would be fantastic if every team member was as understanding and compliant as Steve, but unfortunately that's not always the case. I've had people lash out at me and tell me that I'm the problem. Don't be surprised if you get people who "kick stones" your way. It's inevitable. If you haven't been holding people accountable already, there is a greater chance that some will become unruly when you attempt to harness their harmful behavior.

One time I had a member of my team get in my face and call me out, and I had to handle it in the following way:

"Look, I don't mind your comments, even if you want to get rough and tumble with me, but we're going to respect each other," I said. "Lashing out at me isn't respectful. If you want to voice your opinion, I'm okay with that. However, let's do it by making eye contact and not taking shots at each other or other people who aren't in the room with us. Are we in agreement, or not?"

It won't be easy at first, but the more often you have these conversations, the better you'll get. Remember, the more committed you are to protecting your culture and building an environment of trust, the more respect you'll receive.

You have to trust what you're doing. If you want to straighten and strengthen people's backbones, you'll need to take control of these situations. Expect that when you ask for a commitment to change, some people will flat out tell you, "I don't think I can work in this environment anymore." Perfect—now you know the truth. You can figure out an exit strategy and perhaps a severance, and off they go.

Following Through and Trusting Yourself

One day, I was having lunch with a good friend of mine who had actually been through RedRock Leadership training. As many people often do, he told me that not only did he find value in applying these principles at work, but he also applied them at home. He was, however, in a bit of a conundrum. He had set up core values for his household, and he was spitting angry when his teenage son violated them.

"You have to be careful not to operate from a place of anger, bitterness, or resentment because when you do, your emotions are controlling you. It's not going to end well," I told him. "I want you to get to a place where you're controlling your emotions instead of them controlling you so you can lead your son toward a positive future. Sit down with him and talk about how he's in violation of your family's core values. Lay them out in front of him."

I continued, "Help him understand there are consequences for his actions. Let him know if he isn't willing to comply with your family's core values, you can find a place for him to live outside the home, and he can work to support himself. If he doesn't want that to happen and he wants to stay, ask for his commitment to those core values. Make sure he knows they're not rules, but guidelines put in place to create a safe environment for your family. If he gives you his commitment to change, look him in the eye and tell him that you trust him."

"But I don't trust him," he said.

"But you do because you're allowing him to stay in your home right now. You trust him, but it's masked by emotion," I said. "Don't be permissive and trust, be firm and trust. If he violates those core values again, you have to let him know that it's the last time. Period. End of story."

As our one-hour lunch turned into two, he told me that he was beginning to understand how this approach was necessary and important. He agreed to meet with his son and harness his harmful behavior. As it turns out, his son made a commitment to adhere to his family's core values.

Afterward, my friend admitted that it was one of the most difficult conversations he's ever had with anyone. He also said it was one of the most productive. "It's exactly what my son needed to hear, and I was exactly the one he needed to hear it from," he said.

My friend isn't alone. So often, our biggest problem isn't trusting our family members, co-workers, prospects, or other people in our lives. It's trusting ourselves to follow through and make that difficult decision to cut the cord.

How many times have we let people around us lie, cheat, steal, or mislead us? How often have we held their feet to the fire once we realized their transgressions? Probably not as often as we should. We don't trust ourselves to follow through and deal with the consequences. When there is a breakdown somewhere along the line, we often don't have to look much further than our own ability to make a choice, trust that choice, and see it through to the end of the process.

The Benefit of Difficult Decisions

There's no getting around it—protecting your culture will force you to make difficult decisions. Like I mentioned before, a strong culture will sort out the bad apples, but what do you do if one of those bad apples is your top performer?

That's what happened to Xander, a client of mine who owns an insurance agency. Once we established the company's core values, it turned out that Grace, his number one salesperson, wasn't aligned with them. Xander was upset because Grace purchased personal items with her company credit card on business trips and tried to pass them off as professional expenses. But Grace was bringing in a third of the company's revenue, so Xander let her behavior go on for four years. Four years! What could he possibly do about it now without potentially losing her and doing serious damage to the company?

When the latest expense report came in, he finally told me, "I've had enough!"

"Xander, you learned how to harness harmful behavior in RedRock Leadership training," I said.

"I don't have the guts to do it," he said. At least he was honest.

"Okay, so what do you want to do?"

"Could you help me?"

"Of course," I said.

We met with Grace together, and she immediately knew something was up.

"Why am I here?" she asked.

"You're a key member of the team and doing a great job. You're here because we have to get some things straight and set some parameters, so we can get back on track," Xander said. "I have been observing some inconsistencies with your behavior and our company's core values."

"Where are you getting this from?" she asked, polite but direct.

"The expense reports," Xander explained.

"It's never been an issue before. Why is it an issue now?" she asked.

"It has been an issue, but it was never spoken about before we established these core values," he said. "All I need to know is if you are committed to making some changes to get on the right track." I watched as the two of them had a very productive discussion.

"Can we erase the past and move forward?" Xander asked.

"Absolutely. Thanks for letting me know," she said.

It was settled! Everything was great for about six months when there was another breach. Xander did what he knew he needed to do and eliminated her position. And as he feared, Grace went on to work for his number one competitor—taking some business with her. But do you know what Xander told me when it was all said and done?

"I feel relieved, and even though we lost some business I learned a valuable lesson." And he wasn't the only one who was fed up. There were a lot of other team members who felt Grace's departure was long overdue. Once she was gone, the rest of the organization rallied together to fill the gaps.

Establishing yourself with authority doesn't mean you have to be nasty. You simply have to view it as protecting the rest of the organization. Sometimes, we're only talking about one or two bad apples, which might amount to a small percentage of the people you manage. And remember that when it comes to tossing the bad apples, you'll most likely have the rest of the team cheering you on.

What If Leadership Doesn't Align with the Organization's Core Values?

This can happen, and when it does, I believe in harnessing harmful behavior upward, as tactfully as possible. However, you have to be able to recognize if you're in the right place for this to occur. Some will entertain the conversation, but it's important to be respectful and in the Approach State before diving in.

If you find yourself in a position where you have to confront those at the top, there's a right and a wrong way to do it. Don't start by directly singling out those in leadership for not adhering to the core values. Instead, ease into a conversation and say something like, "I've noticed some inconsistencies in the organization." Wait and see if the door opens for you to continue with a question like, "What do you mean?" Then walk through that door by asking, "Do I have permission to share some things that might be offensive to you?" If they open the next door, walk through it, and proceed as far as you can go.

You might be surprised to find that some will respond by saying, "I didn't realize I had a blind spot. I respect you and want to make some changes. Thanks for bringing it to my attention."

Shortly after Janet, the owner of a fast-growing IT firm, started attending RedRock Leadership training, she established and defined her core values. I suggested that she memorize and internalize them before sharing them with her team, but instead she presented them and decided to post them throughout the office.

Within about three weeks, her marketing manager, who also attended RedRock Leadership training, approached her about some inconsistencies as they related to the core values and some of Janet's actions. The marketing manager had a deep level of respect for Janet and approached her with empathy and consideration. In turn, Janet received the observations and owned up to them. She shared this story with me and was extremely complimentary of the process that helped her accept and deal proactively with one of her blind spots.

Don't be surprised if this conversation goes in the opposite direction, though. There will always be someone who says, "You have no idea what's going on here, or in my life. I need you to go back to doing what you were doing and not worry about what's going on here." And if you want to stay, you have to respect that and learn to live with it or move on.

Mark, the owner of a mid-size packaging company, was nothing at all like Janet, nor was his warehouse manager anything like Janet's marketing manager. After Mark attended RedRock Leadership training, he took some time to internalize his newly developed core values. Shortly after presenting and posting them, Mark was confronted by his warehouse manager, who had been disgruntled for months, about inconsistencies between what he was seeing within the organization and the newly stated core values.

Mark was quick to flip the script on his warehouse manager and asked him if he'd be willing to stand behind the company's newly stated core values and help him lead the charge to create a positive shift in the company culture. The warehouse manager wanted nothing to do with this and didn't feel it was his job to lead the charge. The conversation ended with neither man feeling good about the other. Within 10 days, the warehouse manager resigned.

If you're going to take the initiative to approach leadership, you must remember that they're the ultimate authority within the company. That means that if you're going to stay at the company, you may need to adjust your mindset and perhaps lower your expectations.

Regardless, make sure your personal core values align with the values of your organization, otherwise you've got an integrity issue and you'll struggle to maintain a high enough level of emotional intelligence to succeed there long-term.

Remember, you don't have to stay. You can always move on. Make it a "win/win or walk away" situation. It may help to look at it this way: you are your own business, and the company that gives you your paycheck is your number one client.

Coach and Hold Your Team Accountable

One of leadership's key objectives must be to position everyone on their teams so that they're heading in the same direction toward a positive future. When people in your organization are running in different directions, it creates chaos.

The simplest way to ensure everyone on your team is on track is to provide proactive, ongoing coaching. There are three categories of coaching:

1. **Personal Coaching.** This type of coaching focuses on habits, personal accountability, and intrapersonal skills. Personal awareness, etiquette, and attitude all fall into this category.

2. **Skills Coaching.** This type of coaching focuses on interpersonal skills and day-to-day strategies, including efficiency, time management, and organization.

3. **Performance Coaching.** This is a higher level of coaching for those whom you want to see step up into a leadership role. Performance coaching will help emerging leaders learn

how to develop a vision and strategy as well as systems and processes.

The following pages show how we break down personal coaching plans using the RedRock Coaching Evaluators.™

1. PERSONAL COACHING EVALUATION

RedRock Personal Coaching Evaluator™

0 ←————————————————————————→ 10
Never   Sometimes   Always

Personal Awareness – recognizes influence on others	
_____	Is secure and doesn't use awkward humor, sadness, or anger to cover up insecurities.
_____	Trusts the process and is confident around difficult to manage people and / or tasks.
Integrity – intentions match actions	
_____	Takes personal responsibility when making mistakes.
_____	Is transparent and doesn't bend the truth when under pressure.
Internal Motivation – does the right things for the right reasons	
_____	Thinks of the team before himself or herself.
_____	Is focused on doing the right things for the right reasons, as opposed to constantly avoiding punishment or seeking recognition.
Total Score	
_____	Enter the total of all three areas.

Score:	Action:
0 - 30 Below Average	Personal coaching will help establish a foundation for success.
31 - 48 Average	Personal coaching will help improve personal performance.
49 - 60 Above Average	Personal coaching isn't necessary, but it certainly will not hurt.

2. SKILLS COACHING EVALUATION

RedRock Skills Coaching Evaluator™

0 ◄─────────────────────────────────► 10
Never   Sometimes   Always

Empathy – recognizes and responds well to the emotions of others
____ Co-workers and clients see him or her as a reliable "go-to" person.
____ Relates well to management, co-workers, and clients.
Social Skills – builds positive relationships
____ Makes others feel comfortable with their verbal and non-verbal communication.
____ Is more assertive than aggressive, passive, or passive aggressive.
Total Score
____ Enter the total of both areas.

Score:	Action:
0 - 20 Below Average	Skills coaching will help establish a foundation for success.
21 - 32 Average	Skills coaching will help improve day-to-day performance.
33 - 40 Above Average	Skills coaching isn't necessary, but it certainly will not hurt.

3. PERFORMANCE COACHING EVALUATION

RedRock Performance Coaching Evaluator™

0 ←		→ 10
Never	Sometimes	Always

Vision - the passion pursued
____ Understands and supports the vision of the organization.
____ Is effective at communicating the organization's vision.
Goals - the underlying support to the organization's vision
____ Sets goals that support the organization's vision.
____ Achieves goals that support the organization's vision.
Strategy - the underlying support to the organization's goals
____ Creates and supports the systems and processes that support the organization's goals.
____ Complies with the organization's systems and processes.
Action Steps - underlying support to the organization's strategies
____ Takes ownership of actions and consistently supports the organization's strategies.
____ Supports efforts of continuous improvement within the organization.
Accountability - underlying support to personal action steps
____ Assumes personal responsibility to make the organization better.
____ Consistently completes tasks and projects on time.
Total Score
____ Enter the total of all five areas.

Score:	Action:
0 - 50 Below Average	Performance coaching will help establish a foundation for success.
51 - 80 Average	Performance coaching will help improve strategic performance.
81 - 100 Above Average	Performance coaching isn't necessary, but it certainly will not hurt.

While coaching, it's important to continuously point to a positive future. You want to build your team up with coaching, not knock them down. If you don't remember anything else when it comes to coaching, remember PCP (praise, coach, praise). This is called a motivation sandwich: the outside bun is sweet, and the inside middle is the meat!

Also, please don't overlook the importance of creating coaching plans. It will help you stay organized and monitor progress. I find that when I follow a plan, I'm more likely to listen and assume goodwill rather than just hammer my points home or make a list of to-dos that will only end up sounding like "constructive" criticism, which we know is not a good idea.

Here are the guidelines for coaching:

1. Gather accurate information and be objective.

2. Be specific when providing feedback.

3. Ask questions to promote collaboration.

4. Listen with the intention of understanding.

5. When necessary, provide on-the-job training.

6. Continue dialogue after the meeting while pointing to a positive future.

7. Acknowledge good decisions and commitments to improve.

Your style and language is equally important when it comes to achieving your desired outcome.

- To open the conversation, use open-ended questions that start with "who," "what," "when," "where," "how," and "why." For example, you can ask, "How do you feel about the way things are going?"

- Close-ended questions that begin with "if," "do," "did," "can," "is," and "are" can be a good way to end a conversation. For example, you can ask, "Do you think we're on the same page?"

- Power extraction statements like "tell me more," "please clarify," "be specific," and "show me" allow for a direct approach. For example, you can say, "Show me how you currently do it."

Keep in mind that most people don't want to be told "what" to do as much as they want to know "why" they're doing it. For this reason, open your coaching conversation with something like, "I believe you are a key ingredient to our long-term success." This will answer the all-important question they're already thinking, which is, "Why is this coaching session happening?" When you anticipate their "why," you'll create a connection. If you begin by explaining what you expect from them, you're likely to cause confusion and meet resistance.

Remember that it's not about you. Too many people think that the purpose of coaching is to address problem areas, but that's not entirely true. The main purpose of coaching is to meet your people where they are and point them toward success. I love this quote by John C. Maxwell, author of *The 21 Irrefutable Laws of Leadership*: "A leader is one who knows the way, goes the way, and shows the way."

There's no better way to live this than to roll up your sleeves and assume responsibility for helping the people on your team grow stronger.

CHAPTER 10

HOW TO CREATE AND ACCOMPLISH ACTIONABLE GOALS

I f there is one thing I've learned from coaching and training hundreds of individuals and companies throughout my career, it's this: if you set goals and make plans to accomplish them, you'll excel well beyond those who don't take the time to make this commitment. And if you take the time to measure and track them, you'll go even further.

Creating actionable goals is how you'll demonstrate confidence in your strengths and abilities and put yourself in a position to be held accountable. In addition, the quality of your goal plan will be directly proportionate to your level of success in whatever it is you set out to accomplish.

Why Do We Fail to Accomplish Our Goals?

Let's begin with two simple questions:

1. What is a recent goal you set but didn't accomplish?

2. Why do you believe you didn't accomplish that goal?

Below are a few typical responses:

Goal	Reason It Wasn't Accomplished
Pay off debt	Took a vacation instead
Lose weight	Procrastination
Build a house	Not enough money for a down payment
Learn a foreign language	Bought the program, but never used it

Anytime you fail to accomplish a goal, you can expect that it's because you were lacking in one or more of the following three areas:

1. Vision: Your passion about pursuing it to its end

2. Motivation: Your desire to see it through to fruition, no matter what

3. Plan: Your intention about setting aside time to measure and track your progress

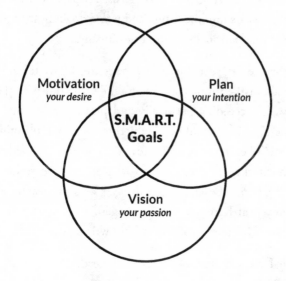

All three of these areas intersect to create S.M.A.R.T. goals. Your goals are not S.M.A.R.T. if you're lacking in any of the following areas:

S – Specific

M – Measurable

A – Attainable

R – Realistic

T – Time-Bound

When I was in my late twenties, I went through a coaching program for entrepreneurs called The Strategic Coach™ by Dan Sullivan. During one segment of that training, I was led through a heavy-duty lesson on goal setting. It was incredibly impactful and helped me create S.M.A.R.T. goals. As part of the exercise, I looked three years into the future and wrote down how I saw myself succeeding first personally, then professionally.

Just about every year since this experience, I have taken the time to think about the future (my vision) and write down all they ways I see myself succeeding personally and professionally (my motivation). Then I write them down in my three-year goal planning guide (my plan). I've even gotten my wife and daughters involved. Because of the effectiveness of this style of goal planning, we've managed to visit all 30 Major League Baseball parks as a family. In addition, we've enjoyed at least one vacation together every year, we built a home, started businesses, and now I am writing this book.

When I created RedRock's Personal Leadership training, I also created the RedRock Three-Year Goal-Planning Guide™, which has become instrumental in helping individuals and companies expand well past where they are when we first meet. I will go into more details about this planning guide a little later on in this chapter.

Leverage Your Time to Accomplish Your Goals

One tabletop discussion I assign to participants during RedRock Leadership training asks them to identify what they would eliminate, on a daily basis, in order to be more productive. If eliminated from your life, what would make you more productive?

Here are the four most popular answers:

1. Busywork

2. Distractions

3.   Interruptions

4.   Ineffective Delegation

This last one is interesting because ineffective delegation can work two ways. For some it means holding on to the tasks they should delegate, and for others it means saying "yes" to everything that comes their way.

Next, I ask the participants to draw pictures of themselves and their relationship with time. Why don't you take a minute to do it? Go ahead, have some fun.

What did you come up with?

I've seen drawings of stick figures arguing with their watch. I've seen sketches of people chasing clocks. One of my all-time favorites was a drawing of a stick figure standing in front of an ATM that dispensed time instead of money; the screen read "zero balance." Now that's funny!

What's sad is that I don't think I've ever seen a picture of someone having fun and enjoying time. Most drawings are an expression of how disappointed and frustrated people are with time. Could you imagine spending 24 hours a day with someone you dread? Our relationship with time isn't unlike our relationship with each other. If we don't invest and nurture our relationship with time, we'll only become frustrated and stressed.

Have you ever taken a time management course? If you have, then you know that if you don't keep up with what you've learned it's a temporary fix. It's a lot like going to counseling to repair a relationship with a loved one. If all you do is use what you learned to manipulate your situation, it's not likely that the relationship will thrive.

The fact is people mistreat that which they don't value or respect. If you don't actually value and respect time, then techniques like starting early and time-blocking become manipulation tactics that you use to try and control it.

Those who experience higher levels of success have learned how to "leverage" in order to get where they want to go. Because of their ability to persevere and trust, they build strong relationships with people whose time, talent, and resources they can leverage to accomplish that which they are not able to accomplish on their own. This same concept relates to leveraging your time to accomplish your goals.

How to Leverage Time

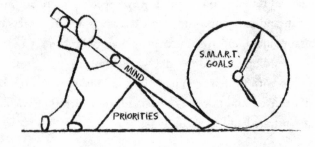

Think about what it means to leverage something. To begin, you need a lever, a fulcrum, and an opposing force.

Suppose your car slid off the road and got stuck in the snow. If you found a dried stick to use as a lever, it would snap. It's the same thing with your fulcrum. If your fulcrum is a pile of sand, it doesn't matter how tightly you pack it, that won't work either.

Think of it like this:

- The LEVER represents YOUR MIND

- The FULCRUM represents YOUR PRIORITIES

- The OPPOSING FORCE represents YOUR S.M.A.R.T. GOALS

As you continue to build and sustain mental toughness, you'll develop a strong mind that will allow you to experience prolonged existence in the Approach State. When you realize balance in all areas of your life, you'll get the most out of time, and your priorities will remain in order. This is when you'll realize goal accomplishment, or as we say at RedRock, this is when you'll unleash the potential for exponential growth!

Michael's Story

Michael, a company manager, conscientiously answers phone calls for much of his day, chatting with customers, coworkers, and superiors. He takes his daily meetings and engagements seriously, listening to his team members' personal problems, often for a good portion of the afternoon.

He interacts with people nonstop, always striving to connect with his customers and team members, and he is constantly in motion, working through customer and team issues. He also meets with vendors throughout the week and gains insight into how to secure materials while saving money. Still, he rarely has time to take advantage of these opportunities because he's so busy.

Between the work on his desk and the time he spends with people, Michael seems to focus fewer hours each month on process improvement. He has a higher customer satisfaction rating than anyone else in the company, and he relies on that rating for management's approval. He has always intended to set his own goals, but he hasn't had time to do it.

Before you continue reading, take some time to think about answers to the following questions:

1. What do you observe about Michael?

2. What recommendations do you have for Michael?

The first common observation is that Michael has always intended to set goals for himself, but just hasn't taken the time to actually do it. It's also easy to see that Michael struggles in the area of emotional intelligence, specifically his intrapersonal skills, personal awareness, integrity, and internal motivation. Even if you're an avid goal setter, you probably notice some of your own tendencies in Michael's story. Doesn't it seem like it's becoming increasingly more challenging to navigate through the furious pace that exists today?

If you're interested in a proven approach that has helped many people, including me, get out from underneath a reactive lifestyle and get into a position where you can focus on the future while being proactive every day, look no further than The RedRock Leadership 4-Step Personal Growth Plan.™

The RedRock Leadership 4-Step Personal Growth Plan

1. **Align Each Area of Your Life with Your Core Values.** In order to pursue your personal and professional desires, you must first have a clear understanding of your priorities. When your priorities are in order, you'll be less likely to get distracted. Here are the seven key areas of life:

- Family

- Health

- Education

- Work

- Faith

- Social

- Finance

Now, take some time and rearrange them so they're in order from most to least important to you, and then grade yourself on how fulfilled you feel in those areas. The more honest you are with yourself, the more you'll get out of this exercise.

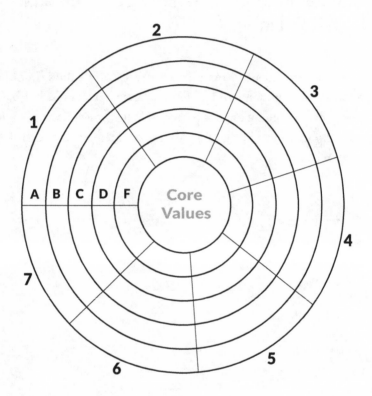

Next, place your core values in the center of the wheel. Remember your core values are the fundamental principles and beliefs that guide your actions and behavior. They represent the hub that supports the seven areas of your life and keep you balanced.

Now, insert each of the areas of your life on this wheel in accordance with how you ranked them (one, two, three, etc.). Next shade each segment of the wheel from the inside out based on how you graded yourself. So, if you gave yourself an A for the area you ranked first, then shade that entire segment from the inside all the way out, and so on with each segment.

What are you observing about your shaded wheel? Some say, "It's no wonder my ride through life seems so bumpy," while others say, "I see now why life seems to be moving so fast."

The lower the grades you give yourself, the smaller the wheel gets. This would explain why life seems to be moving so fast. The higher the grades you give yourself, the larger the wheel gets. This is when life begins to slow down a bit. You would be okay if life slowed down a little, wouldn't you? Slowing your pace is a key ingredient to raising your EQ.

One of the secrets to getting life to go a little slower is to be more intentional, but we're all busy and in a hurry, which is how we end up shortchanging ourselves. Maybe you want to improve your health. You might want to go back to school. Do you have a loved one with whom you want to spend a little more time? If you're not intentional, you can find yourself robbing one area of your life to pay for another. This can put unnecessary pressure on you and result in unintended consequences.

If your journey through life is bumpy and you're out of balance, first look at your actions and behaviors and their misalignment with your core values. This misalignment will be reflected in how you grade each area of your life. This will help you identify relationships that aren't working, business objectives that aren't being attained, and goals that aren't being accomplished.

You'll be able to accomplish your goals when your actions and behaviors align with your core values and you're getting A's and B's in all areas of your life.

2. Get Your Priorities in Order. If you want to ensure that your actions and behaviors remain in alignment with your core values and that you continue to score A's and B's in all areas of your life, I strongly recommend implementing the RedRock Priority Stabilizer.™ You can download it and begin using it today at RedRockLeadership.com/the-book.

RedRock Priority Stabilizer™

	Monday	Tuesday	Wednesday	Thursday	Friday	Saturday	Sunday
4:00 AM	Sleep	Sleep	Sleep	Sleep	Sleep	Sleep	Sleep
5:00 AM	Faith	Faith	Faith	Faith	Faith	Faith	Faith
6:00 AM	Faith	Faith	Faith	Faith	Faith	Faith	Faith
7:00 AM	Health	Health	Health	Health	Health	Health	Faith
8:00 AM	Focus/Work	Focus/Work	Focus/Work	Focus/Work	Education	Family	Faith
9:00 AM	Focus/Work	Focus/Work	Focus/Work	Focus/Work	Education	Family	Faith
10:00 AM	Focus/Work	Focus/Work	Focus/Work	Focus/Work	Education	Family	Faith
11:00 AM	Focus/Work	Focus/Work	Focus/Work	Focus/Work	Admin/Work	Family	Faith
12:00 PM	Focus/Work	Focus/Work	Focus/Work	Focus/Work	Admin/Work	Family	Faith
1:00 PM	Focus/Work	Focus/Work	Focus/Work	Focus/Work	Admin/Work	Family	Faith
2:00 PM	Focus/Work	Focus/Work	Focus/Work	Focus/Work	Admin/Work	Family	Family
3:00 PM	Focus/Work	Focus/Work	Focus/Work	Focus/Work	Admin/Work	Family	Family
4:00 PM	Focus/Work	Focus/Work	Focus/Work	Focus/Work	Admin/Work	Family	Family
5:00 PM	Focus/Work	Focus/Work	Focus/Work	Focus/Work	Family	Family	Family
6:00 PM	Family	Social	Faith	Financial	Family	Family	Family
7:00 PM	Family	Social	Faith	Family	Family	Family	Family
8:00 PM	Family	Social	Faith	Family	Family	Family	Family
9:00 PM	Family	Social	Family	Family	Family	Family	Family
10:00 PM	Sleep	Sleep	Sleep	Sleep	Sleep	Sleep	Sleep
11:00 PM	Sleep	Sleep	Sleep	Sleep	Sleep	Sleep	Sleep
12:00 AM	Sleep	Sleep	Sleep	Sleep	Sleep	Sleep	Sleep
1:00 AM	Sleep	Sleep	Sleep	Sleep	Sleep	Sleep	Sleep
2:00 AM	Sleep	Sleep	Sleep	Sleep	Sleep	Sleep	Sleep
3:00 AM	Sleep	Sleep	Sleep	Sleep	Sleep	Sleep	Sleep

Faith	24	14%
Family	35	21%
Financial	1	1%
Focus/Work	40	24%
Admin/Work	6	4%
Health	6	4%
Education	3	2%
Social	4	2%
Sleep	49	29%
Total Hours	**168**	

Two years after I started my own business, a friend offered to sell me a life insurance policy, so I filled out all the paperwork and took a blood test. A few days later, I got a disturbing call from him.

"I can't give you all the details because I don't have the results, but you need to see a doctor," he said.

"What do you mean?"

"All I know is they won't approve you. You've been deemed high-risk. They told us to tell you to go see your doctor."

What's interesting is that I'll put tasks off for days if they're un-important to me. But it took me all of two minutes to schedule that doctor's appointment. And as it turned out, I had high cholesterol.

"It must be hereditary," I said.

"Does anyone in your family have high cholesterol?" the doctor asked.

"I don't think so."

"Then it's not hereditary. Tell me about your lifestyle."

"Well, I eat well and work out."

I'll let you in on a little secret: I didn't eat well or work out. My lifestyle then was much different than it is today. I didn't let on to that at first, but the doctor could see right through me. Once he started peeling back the onion, we finally got to the heart of the issue: lack of sleep.

Back then, I'd come home from work to eat dinner with my fam-ily, and then I'd put on a pot of coffee and work until about 2 a.m. I'd take a two-hour nap, get up, and start working before I went into the office the next morning. I did that consistently for about two years.

When I finally came clean with the doctor, he gave me a stern talking to. In effect, he harnessed my harmful behavior.

"Let me help you understand something about how the human body works," he said. "Your body is programmed to regenerate by producing growth hormones between midnight and 2:30 a.m. If you're not sleeping during those hours, your body will have some-thing to say about it. Your liver won't metabolize sugar properly, which leads to all sorts of health problems." By the time we finished talking, I was committed to getting on the right track.

I'm a fixer, so I logged on to my computer and created a spreadsheet, which I often do when I get stressed. I wanted to recreate the structure of my week. I proceeded to take my cursor and highlight 24 rows for 24 hours, and I then highlighted seven columns for seven days. I looked in the bottom right hand corner of my screen, and there it was—the number 168. That was the first time I realized there were 168 hours in a week.

How would I fit everything I wanted and needed to do into those 168 hours, while still taking care of myself and making sure to sleep? That led me to create the RedRock Priority Stabilizer, a tool designed to get every area of your life in order. If you're stressed out and things aren't going the way you want them to go, you can refer back to this tool as a guide to bring you back to a place of stability.

3. Accept the RedRock Three-Year Goal-Planning Challenge.™

Dreams and desires only become reality when you write them down and turn them into goals. Once you can measure and track your goals, they become a vital part of the strategic foundation for success in your personal and professional life.

Here is all you have to do to accept the RedRock Three-Year Goal-Planning Challenge:

1. Go to RedRockLeadership.com/the-book and accept the challenge. You'll receive your RedRock Three-Year Goal-Planning Guide.

2. Within three days of accepting the challenge, set aside two to three hours to be alone and quiet.

3. Follow the format outlined in the RedRock Three-Year Goal-Planning Guide and write down 50 goals you want to accomplish in the next three years. Be specific, using dates, dollars, and other details.

4. Share your goals with someone who will encourage you and hold you accountable.

5. Refer to the RedRock Three-Year Goal Planning Guide at least monthly to measure and track your progress.

4. **Complete the RedRock Leveraging Time Battlecard.**™ The RedRock Leveraging Time Battlecard is modeled after the four-quadrants inspired by Benjamin Franklin and popularized by the author Stephen Covey. This tool helps you be ultra-clear about the activities and tasks you must focus on to maximize goal accomplishment.

You can download and personalize your own RedRock Leveraging Time Battlecard at RedRockLeadership.com/the-book.

RedRock Leveraging Time Battlecard™

QUADRANT 2:

Let's begin with the "do it" quadrant, which means that these are things that only you can do. This is your wheelhouse. This is the "important, but not urgent" quadrant. Start by writing down the top three to five tasks and activities for which you are directly responsible.

QUADRANT 3:

This is the "ditch it or delegate it" quadrant. There is no "do it" here, which means these are tasks and activities that you're involved in but not responsible for. These can be activities that others dump on you—the things that are in your lane but probably shouldn't be there. These may actually be stressors that cause you to slip into the Avoid State because you feel nobody will do these tasks if you don't.

QUADRANT 4:

This is the quadrant for your "bad habits." These are the things that were once in quadrant three but have become permanent fixtures in your life. They could be anything from partying, social media, or smoking, which I consider to be one of the greatest time wasters ever and one of the worst decisions someone could possibly make.

It's not easy to just cut these activities out of your life because they've become so deeply ingrained. It might require the help of a coach or a counselor. Be honest with yourself when writing down all of the bad habits that waste your precious time.

QUADRANT 1:

This quadrant is often misunderstood, which makes it a fun topic to discuss. This quadrant encompasses "do it or delegate it" tasks or activities. Let's say I'm in the middle of a RedRock Leadership training session when I get a call from Craig, who needs my advice on how to handle an emergency with team members. I either need to leave the training session to deal with it or delegate the task to someone else in my company. Leaving the class is not a good idea, but what I could do is have the group take 10 minutes to work on an exercise while I step away to speak with Craig. I take a moment to assess the situation, figure out whether I should "do it or delegate it," and then return to the class.

It's important to keep a high level of personal awareness when dealing with these tasks because time stressors are notorious for landing us in the Avoid State. I saw that happen once when I was in the middle of a meeting. A guy across the room read a text then grabbed his belongings and bolted out of the room. We all thought someone died, but we later learned he had just forgotten about a conference call.

I'm forgetful, so I know what that feels like, but there's a much better way to handle that situation. He could have explained what had happened to those in the meeting, excused himself, and then figured out how to handle the conference call or delegated the task to someone else. Panic never leads anywhere good.

I encourage you to implement the RedRock Leveraging Time Battlecard to help you remain accountable to only working on tasks that support your goals and only focusing on activities for which you are directly responsible.

CHAPTER 11

PROTECT YOUR RELATIONSHIP WITH TIME

N ot many people realize there are 168 hours in a week. I went the first 35 years of my life never thinking about it. How can we just meander through life not recognizing something so important?

Picture going out to a restaurant for a meal with your family, then handing over your debit card to pay without knowing if you have enough in your bank account to cover the check. That's crazy. But most people do this every day with their time.

Time is every human being's single greatest non-replenishable resource. Think about it. It's not possible to save, invest, or borrow time. However, it is possible to use time more effectively. Success is contingent on setting goals and allocating quality time against highly leveraged activities to accomplish these goals.

There's an old story about a professor who did a demonstration for his students. He started with a big jar and filled it with large rocks. He asked the students if the jar was full, and they agreed that it was full. Then he dumped some pebbles into the jar, shook it lightly, and watched the pebbles settle into the open areas between the rocks. He asked again if the jar was full, and the students said it was. He then poured sand into the jar, and the sand filled the open areas between the rocks and pebbles. He looked at the students and said, "*Now* the jar is full."

How can you apply this to your life?

- The JAR represents the 168 hours in your week.

- The ROCKS symbolize your priorities and goals—the truly important things. If you lost everything else and only the rocks remained, you would be fulfilled.

- The PEBBLES are the other things in your life that matter, including day-to-day important to-dos. They're important, but not crucial. They are items that can and ought to be scheduled.

- The SAND is all the small stuff like tending to email and paperwork. If you're not careful, they can keep you from giving attention to the rocks and pebbles.

If you were to put sand in the jar first, there would be no room for the rocks or pebbles. Translation: If you spend all your time and energy on the small stuff, you will never have room for the things that are truly important. There will always be time to clean the house, work late, or worry about the little things. Take care of the rocks first. Establish your priorities, set your goals, and protect your time. The rest is just pebbles and sand.

Front-Load to Manage Expectations

A good strategy for leveraging your time is front-loading. Think about it, when your expectations aren't being met, you get frustrated, and when you get frustrated, everything breaks down. You become less motivated, lack perseverance, stop trusting, and your EQ drops. Front-loading is a technique you can use to bring the future to the present by setting expectations about what can happen next. Front-loading is also a way to prioritize important tasks and activities before the day or week begins. It's an effective strategy to leverage your time, and it goes hand-in-hand with managing activities and tasks in your time quadrants.

The idea behind front-loading is learning how to prioritize guidelines for communication before an important conversation or a meeting. It will help you establish yourself as a leader. It's simple and requires three steps:

1. **Communicate your purpose.** The idea is to begin with empathy and consideration. Don't just lay out rules and demands. That's not the way it works. You want to keep other people's feelings in mind when you explain why you want to meet or have a discussion. You might say something like, "I have a few ideas that might help things run a little smoother. I'd like to talk with you about it."

2. **Ensure you have enough time.** Make sure you let the other person, or group, know how much time it will take to talk through what you want to discuss. To ensure you have enough time, you could say something like, "This conversation won't take more than 30 minutes, are we good?" It's better to move a conversation to a time when you have the

other person's full attention instead of having to rush, cut yourself short, and not be able to make your point or hear their ideas.

3. **Outline possible outcomes.** Don't beat around the bush and don't rush to judgment. Instead, share the possible results of your meeting or discussion before you get started. For example, you could say, "When we're finished meeting, I'd like us to create a few action items along with due dates or if we aren't quite ready for that, we can set up another meeting to continue our discussion." Don't forget to end with empathy and consideration by saying something along the lines of, "Are you okay with all of this? Do you have any comments or questions before we get started?"

Front-loading can work a lot of different ways and for a lot of different scenarios. Let's say that you're going into a meeting but know you might have to leave if you get a particular call. Instead of startling everyone by walking out during the middle of the meeting, let the others in the meeting know about the situation ahead of time so there are no surprises. You can say, "I may get a call at 10:30 and need to step out for 15 minutes." Rarely will anyone have a problem with it. In fact, you're likely to gain respect when you minimize frustrations because you're establishing expectations in advance.

If you're on the phone and pressed for time, you might say something as simple as, "I just want to let you know I only have about 10 minutes left on this call before I have to go." That will help you manage the expectations of everyone involved.

A few years ago, I had the chance to present a leadership training proposal to an executive team of a large company I greatly respected.

I wanted to make sure I managed their expectations because there was a lot on the line.

I started with empathy and consideration.

"I've known of your company for years, and I appreciate the opportunity to meet with you today," I said. "I know that our meeting invitation indicates that we have until 3:30 Is everyone still good with this?"

The president of the company stepped up and said, "Actually, I have a hard stop at 3:15."

That's something I would not have known had I not front-loaded, but once I knew, I could adjust accordingly. This kept everyone in the Approach State.

This technique can work in any area of your life. There have been plenty of times when I've needed to establish expectations in advance with my wife and have said something like, "Just an FYI, but I have an extremely crazy day and then a dinner meeting, so you probably won't hear from me much today. I won't be home for dinner, but I'll check in around 2 o'clock and promise to be home by 10 o'clock."

This makes things so much easier. Back in the day, I'd forget to mention something to my wife, and then I'd get a concerned phone call with her asking, "Where are you? Are you coming home?"

"Oh, I forgot to tell you. I have to work late."

She'd be frustrated, and rightfully so.

Whether at work or at home, front-loading is important when it comes to collaboration and making sure everyone is on the same page. To front-load, you need a high level of cognitive empathy to see what's going on around you. That's where starting and ending with empathy and consideration comes into play.

You can also front-load your day or week. This will help you identify urgent and important issues so that you can manage expectations accordingly. When I first started my business, I didn't have much in the way of support. In those days, I learned to set aside time on Friday afternoons to front-load the following week, which helped me allocate quality time against highly leveraged activities so that I could complete my projects on time. If you want to be a leader and improve your time efficiency and effectiveness, I strongly suggest learning how to front-load. Believe me, it works!

CHAPTER 12

CREATE YOUR LEGACY

R edRock Leadership is all about ongoing reinforcement. There
is no one-size-fits-all solution or quick fix. Development and
improvement are part of a constant, ongoing process that helps you
continue to improve yourself and your business over time.

There will always be more ways to learn and grow because un-
anticipated issues and problems will continue to pop up. Just when
you think you have it all figured out, the market shifts, your top
salesperson leaves, or your company is sold. But if you've taken the
time to create the structural foundation you and your company need
for sustainability and leveraged the principles and strategies laid out
in this book, you'll remain relevant through ups and downs.

Not long ago, J-TEK experienced their own set of growing pains,
and the company's leadership team was put to the test. Monica had
been successfully leading the sales team without Craig's day-to-day
involvement for almost a year when there was an unexpected shift in
the market. As a result, the team fell short of their quarterly revenue
and gross profit expectations. Monica was frustrated and began
thinking about replacing some of the salespeople.

Both sales and profits were about 20 percent below what Craig
expected, and Monica wondered how Craig might react to this,

so she came up with a plan. She approached Craig with what she thought he might like to hear and told him she was going to be brutally honest with the team.

"I'm going to lay it on the line and let the team know that they must get their numbers up or staff changes are imminent," she said.

As Craig listened to Monica, he saw Monica was responding from the Avoid State. He was equally as concerned but was able to manage his emotions, which meant he was residing in the Approach State. He didn't get angry or lose his cool as he may have done before we started working together.

Clearly, Craig's level of personal awareness had increased over time because what happened next was nothing short of amazing. He pulled his "RedRock Guidelines for Coaching" laminated card out of a desk drawer and began by answering what Monica's anticipated "why" might be.

"Monica, you are my Plan A, and I don't have a Plan B," he said. "What I mean is that you are the one I want leading this sales team through good times and bad. You're a big reason why we've been able to accomplish what we've accomplished over the past year."

He went on to follow his RedRock guidelines for coaching:

1. Gather accurate information and be objective.

"Monica, there is no question that the numbers are down, but let's look at the facts," Craig said. "Everyone's sales numbers are down, but the prospecting activity that's being reported by the team in CRM remains strong."

2. Be specific when providing feedback.

"I can remember a time when I would have panicked over a drop in sales or profit, but I've learned it's healthier for all involved if I focus on the horizon and look at the bigger picture," he said. "Monica, you've done a fantastic job over the past year. I trust you, and your team trusts you. Now's not the time to be desperate and discouraged."

3. Ask questions to promote collaboration.

"What is it that's really bothering you with all of this? Talk to me," Craig said.

"Craig, I don't want to let you down," Monica replied. "We've come too far, and I feel like the team isn't as motivated or focused as they were six months ago."

4. Listen with the intention of understanding.

"Monica, do you think it's possible that this shift in the market has them concerned as well?" Craig asked.

Monica went on to explain that they were probably frustrated, too. As she continued to talk it out, she came to realize that as the numbers started to slip, her level of perseverance slipped as well and she began to trust them less, which led to their reaction. She also recognized that her level of personal awareness dropped, and she had drifted into the Avoid State and wasn't approaching the team in a way that was inspiring or encouraging.

5. When necessary, provide on-the-job training.

"Monica, rather than me stepping in to handle this situation, let me ask you, do you remember how Jeff Ruby suggested we approach Ronnie and Cindy when they were in their slump late last year?" Craig asked.

"I do," she said. "And I still can't believe you agreed to give the two of them $100 so they could blow off a Friday afternoon right in the midst of their sales slump."

"I know, but do you remember what happened next?" he responded.

"I do," she said. "They both broke out of their slump in the next month, and they've continued to thrive since."

6. Continue dialogue after the meeting while pointing to a positive future.

"That was a turning point for me, Monica," Craig said. "It was at that point that I realized nobody was showing up to fail. Sometimes when a storm comes, you just have to wait for it to pass, and while you're waiting, find a way to focus your attention on something other than the storm."

Craig and Monica role-played a couple of scenarios, and Craig referenced his RedRock Leadership training to help Monica sharpen her empathy skills until she felt ready to address the team with courage and consideration.

"I get it!" she said. "I know exactly what I need to do. Thank you, Craig!"

7. Acknowledge good decisions and commitments to improve.

"I know you get it Monica. I trust you," Craig said. "Like I said, you are my Plan A, and I don't have a Plan B. I appreciate your willingness to guide this sales team in the right direction."

The very next Friday afternoon, Monica brought in ice cream and addressed her team. She told them shifts in the market and dips in results happen from time to time. More importantly, she told them she trusted them to continue to persevere and that they were the right team for the job.

They had a few laughs together and even exchanged a couple of sales war stories. Her team wasn't the problem. She had the right team in place; she just needed to work out the messaging necessary to encourage and inspire her people so they could remain in the Approach State while the storm passed.

It was an interesting journey for J-TEK International, to say the least, but Craig and his team managed to get the company growing in the right direction. He no longer feels the pressure from his father. He no longer blames his team or passes the buck because he's now focused on a positive future. I'm proud of Craig, and I'm grateful to have had a front row seat to see him create his legacy by encouraging and inspiring others.

I'm also grateful that I can consistently play a small part in helping turn companies around. It never gets old! I'd welcome the opportunity to see you do the same. If you'd like to learn more about how RedRock Leadership can help you grow your company by growing your people, please go to RedRockLeadership.com/the-book, complete the contact form, and one of our trusted advisors will contact you right away.

We look forward to helping you transform your company culture and unleash the potential for exponential growth!

DID YOU ENJOY THIS BOOK?

Be sure to share it with your friends and colleagues! Also, if you are interested in having me speak at an upcoming event, please visit RedRockLeadership.com, call my office at 813-885-5097, or send us an email at Training@RedRockLeadership.com.

I look forward to helping you unleash the potential for exponential growth!

Jeff Ruby

CPSIA information can be obtained
at www.ICGtesting.com
Printed in the USA
JSHW022326140622
26835JS00003B/4